The Living Word of the Bible

Bernhard W. Anderson

D0958779

The Westminster Press
Philadelphia

First edition

Published by The Westminster Press ®
Philadelphia, Pennsylvania

PRINTED IN THE UNITED STATES OF AMERICA

9 8 7 6 5 4 3 2 1

Library of Congress Cataloging in Publication Data

Anderson, Bernhard W
   The living word of the Bible.

   A series of lectures originally presented at
theological seminaries in the U.S. and Canada.
   Includes bibliographical references.
   1. Bible—Evidences, authority, etc.—Addresses,
essays, lectures. 2. Bible—Inspiration—Addresses,
essays, lectures. 3. Word of God (Theology)—Addresses, essays, lectures. I. Title.
BS480.A64   220.1   78-27108
ISBN 0-664-24247-2

To
Murray Lee Newman, Jr.

Contents

Preface

In the preface to a published collection of sermons, Harry Emerson Fosdick, minister of Riverside Church in New York City for many years, observed that sermons—unlike the proverbial child of former generations—should be heard, not seen. This remark also applies to the genre of the lecture which is related essentially to an oral "situation in life" where a teacher speaks and students, at least some of the time, listen. Knowing the difference between the spoken and the written word, I have been hesitant to allow the following lectures to be seen in print; I have yielded to persuasion only under the condition that the informal discourse in which they were originally heard should be preserved insofar as possible.

The subject of these lectures is the Bible as "Word of God," a subject that has been at the center of my theological concern since the beginning of my ministry and which, more years ago than I care to stipulate, was addressed in *Rediscovering the Bible*. In the intervening years, which include the tumultuous '60s, the subject has become increasingly problematic, as biblical scholarship has been plunged into controversies about methodology and inevitably has been affected by the rapidly

changing cultural situation. Indeed, some would main-
tain that "word of God" language is dead, except for
those who anachronistically cling to old-fashioned
views of biblical inspiration. Despite the changes that
have taken place, however, the subject is as fundamental and inescapable as ever, especially on Sunday morn-
ings when the church bells ring, as they have through
the centuries, and the believing and worshiping community gathers to "hear the Word of God."

The main body of this book is a series of three lectures, on "Word of Imagination," "Word of Narration," and "Word of Liberation," which were originally
commissioned to be given under the Alexander Clinton
Zabriskie Lectureship at Virginia Theological Seminary. I wish to thank Dean G. Cecil Woods, Jr., and the
members of the seminary community for the wonderful
reception that was given on the occasion of the delivery
of the lectures, February 27–28, 1978. The lectures
were also given in advance, October 31 to November 1,
1977, as the Frances Youngker Vosburgh Lectures at
the Theological School of Drew University. To Presi-
dent Paul Hardin, Dean James Kirby, and the faculty
I extend my thanks for making the occasion a pleasant
and renewing "homecoming." To these three lectures
has been added a fourth, on "Word of Obligation,"
dealing with the theme of biblical faith and political
responsibility, which was presented as the Divinity Day
Lecture on October 28, 1975, at McMaster Divinity
College, Hamilton, Ontario. To the members of the
faculty, and especially to the host on the occasion, my
friend Professor Gerald G. Harrop, I express my gratitude for the invitation to take part in a festive occasion.

There are others who deserve thanks for assistance
in the publication of these lectures: Ruth A. Anderson,

who helped immensely at the first literary stage; Carol
and Kenneth Hanawalt, who carefully edited the final
manuscript; and the staff of The Westminster Press,
who believed that the lectures should reach a wider
audience and offered the cooperation of a publisher.
Last but by no means least, I express my appreciation
to Murray L. Newman, professor of Old Testament at
Virginia Theological Seminary, to whom this book is
affectionately dedicated. Ever since our dialogic en-
counters in Heidelberg, Germany, during a sabbatical
leave in 1958, we have vigorously discussed the issues
dealt with in these lectures as well as many other con-
troversial topics and yet have remained the best of
friends.

Consonant with the purpose of the Zabriskie and
Vosburgh Lectureships, these lectures are addressed
primarily to the church. It is my hope that publication
of them will have the effect of drawing others—ministers and laypersons—into the ongoing theological conversation about the Bible as Word of God.

BERNHARD W. ANDERSON

Princeton Theological Seminary

One

Word of Imagination

While traveling recently in Great Britain, my wife and I came to a charming village in Wales called Hay-on-Wye, where we found lodging in a quaint old inn. To our surprise, we were offered "The Cromwell Room" —the very room in which Oliver Cromwell is said to have stayed during his siege of the castle. To church historians I must confess that we did not go out of our way to follow Cromwell's movements or to sleep where Cromwell slept! Rather, I had heard that the village on the Wye River is famous for its bookshops. The sale of books, new and old, is the major business there. One bookseller has at least ten shops, and his chief competitor may boast an equal number. Needless to say, a whole village devoted to books is an irresistible attraction to a professor—like honey to a bear!

In one shop dealing with used books my eye fell on a title in the Old Testament section: *Modern Criticism and the Preaching of the Old Testament.* Published in 1901, the book contains the 1899 Lyman Beecher Lectures at Yale University by George Adam Smith. The title was as up-to-date as this morning's newspaper. And I knew the author through other writings, such as his commentary on The Book of Isaiah and on the

Twelve Prophets—works that are still worth reading.
So I snatched the book from the shelf and purchased it
for fifty pence. In George Adam Smith the scholar and the preacher
were felicitously united. The famous Scottish divine
was educated at the University of Edinburgh, at New
College (where today one sees an imposing statue of
John Knox), and at the universities of Tübingen and
Leipzig. For a decade after his graduate studies he was
minister of Queen's Cross Free Church (1882–1892).
From the pastorate he was called to be professor of Old
Testament Language, Literature, and Theology at the
United Free College of Glasgow. Later (1909–1935) he
was principal and vice-chancellor of Aberdeen University,
during which time he was knighted (1916) and
became chaplain to the king in Scotland (1933).
Throughout his entire professional career (he died in
1942), Sir George Adam Smith put at the center of his
scholarly concern the task of preaching.

In the course of his lectures on preaching from the
Old Testament, Smith made an astounding claim.
"Modern Criticism," he declared, "has won its war
against the Traditional Theories [of divine authorship
of Scripture]" and "it only remains to discuss the in-
demnity" (*Modern Criticism,* pp. 72–73). That claim
was made at the beginning of this century. But toward
the end of the twentieth century we all know that it is
not just a matter of paying the costs of war, for the war
is still going on—at least in large enclaves in the land.
Not long ago Harold Lindsell published a book, *The
Battle for the Bible,* in which he maintained that biblical inerrancy is "the most important theological topic
of this age." If you doubt that the "War of the Word"
is still raging, read the pages of *Christianity Today,* a

widely read evangelical magazine; or consider the papal ecclesiasticism of the Rev. J. A. O. Preuss, which has led to a split in the Missouri Synod of the Lutheran Church and the exile of a whole theological faculty, now reconstituted as Seminex (Seminary in Exile). Since the time of Sir George Adam Smith's Lyman Beecher Lectures much theological water has gone under the bridge, and many theological bridges have gone under the water! There has been a retrenchment from the line of defense that Smith advocated: the view that Scripture represents an evolving movement from tribal religion through the ethical monotheism of the prophets to the maturity of God's educative process in the New Testament. Yet Smith's concern for the embattled pastor and for biblical preaching is one that I share. Even today, as in his time, many ministers are paralyzed before powerful forces more formidable than Cromwell's armies and, at times, they seem to hear the signal for full-scale retreat.

THE WORD OF GOD IN HUMAN WORDS

So we must ask with George Adam Smith: How are Christians today to understand the Bible as Word of God? This question does not meet us merely at the level of theological debate; it confronts us in the situation of worship. In most churches the reading of Scripture, whether from the Old Testament or the New, is prefaced with the announcement, "Hear the Word of God," though sometimes the imperative is attenuated to "Listen for the Word of God" (a subtle, but significant modulation!). In the service of the Episcopal Church, for instance, reading from Scripture—and this may

apply to the Old Testament as well as the New—is
concluded with the formula, "The Word of the Lord,"
to which the congregation responds, "Thanks be to
God." Furthermore, when ministers stand in the pulpit
they are under the obligation of their ordination to
"preach the Word." These aspects of worship have special significance in the Protestant tradition which
reaches back to the time when Reformers stood on the
conviction *sola scriptura,* "scripture alone," as the
source and criterion of Christian life, worship, and theology. But what do we mean? Is the formula "Word of
God" only a holdover from the past? Is it only a liturgical convention that we recite with tongue in cheek?

On sober reflection, most of us would want to clarify
our intention in using this formulaic language. We
would say, first of all, that "Word of God" is metaphorical language to refer to God's establishing a personal,
I-thou relationship with his people. God's Word is not
to be equated with human words which, as in the case
of the words of this lecture, are conveyed on sound
waves (and later in print) and in the syntax of a particular language, the English language in this case but originally in Hebrew, Aramaic, or Greek. The language of
worship is metaphorical. God's ways are not our ways;
yet insofar as he enters into relationship with his people,
he "speaks" and we are invited to answer. And sec-
ondly, we say that the Bible, through which God enters
into personal relationship with people, is "Word of God
in human words." God does not communicate in the
tongues of angels or in a mysterious code beyond our
ken; he communicates (speaks) through the medium of
very human words—words that we can understand because they are expressive of our human existence, relationships, and history.

Modern biblical criticism has helped us to understand the humanity of the Word of God in the Bible. It has taught us that Scripture is historically conditioned: its words are the words of human beings who lived in particular times, who acted and thought in the sociological context of their society, who were immersed in the wider culture of the ancient Near East. It has taught us that Scripture is not a monolithic whole but, rather, presents a wonderful wealth of human diversity and theological pluralism. It has taught us that much of what is related in Scripture should not be regarded as straightforward history, in the modern sense, but must be regarded as legend, saga, and poetry.

George Adam Smith spoke for many people in the twentieth century when he declared that modern biblical criticism has been a liberating power. It has enabled Christians to say with Augustine, "I believe in order that I may understand," and has emancipated many people from obscurantism and from a sacrifice of the intellect. But modern criticism also poses a dilemma for faith—the very faith that seeks understanding and integrity in the modern world. For the critical approach has shown us so clearly the humanity of Scripture that it is difficult to speak of the Bible as Word of God. Many people today who want to be "honest to God," rather than using stale clichés or, ostrichlike, hiding their heads in the sand during the storm, are driven to the conclusion stated by James Barr in his book *The Bible in the Modern World* (p. 120):

> My account of the formation of the biblical tradition is an account of a *human* work. It is man's statement of his beliefs, the events he has experienced, the stories he has been told, and so on. It has long been customary to align

the Bible with concepts like Word of God, or revelation, and one effect of this has been to align the Bible with a movement *from God to man*. It is man who developed the biblical tradition and man who decided when it might be suitably fixed and made canonical. If one wants to use the Word-of-God type language, the proper terms for the Bible would be Word of Israel, Word of some leading Christians.

The theological problem of how the Bible is "Word of God in human words" applies to the whole of Scripture, Old Testament and New Testament. Some measure of comfort would be provided if we could say that some parts of Scripture (selected psalms, parts of prophetic literature, the Gospels, and some of Paul's letters) fall under the category "Word of God," while other parts are purely human (say, The Book of Joshua, the imprecatory psalms, the pessimistic Ecclesiastes, and some parts of the New Testament). In practice, most people operate with a "canon" within the Canon. But a pick-and-choose approach to Scripture does not ease the theological problem in the slightest. There is no razor sharp enough to separate Word of God from human words—even in those parts of the Bible which we prefer or which are selected as church lectionary. Of the canonical Scriptures it is said: *Omnia ex Deo, omnia ex hominibus* ("All things are from God, all things are from human beings").

Toward the end of the twentieth century, then, we face the very question that Sir George Adam Smith raised at its beginning. In the face of modern biblical criticism, how can we preach with the conviction that the Bible is "Word of God in human words"?

THE WORD OF GOD AS SCRIPTURE

In dealing with this question, one ventures out onto ground whereon even angels would fear to tread! Karl Barth, whom some would regard as a "theological angel" (if not while in this world, then surely in the world beyond), has provided some helpful theological distinctions. At the beginning of his *Dogmatik* (*Church Dogmatics* I/1, pp. 98–140), he distinguishes three separate, but interrelated, forms of the Word of God. The primary form is Jesus Christ, the Word—though perhaps one may be permitted to expand in a more theocentric manner: God's self-disclosure in Israel's history that reaches its climax in Jesus Christ. The second form is Scripture, that is, the Word as written, Holy Writ. And the third form is the preached Word, that is, the proclamation of the church that elicits the faith response of the worshiping congregation and becomes Word of God now *for me, for us.* Notice how these three forms are combined in the section of the Constitution of The United Presbyterian Church in the U.S.A. under the rubric "Directory for Worship" (18.031):

The preached Word, or sermon, not only is based upon the written Word, but is properly and regularly an exposition of Scripture. Through the sermon, God makes such use as he determines of the words of humans, to confront his children with the saving Word, which is his Son. The preaching of the Word is that act of worship through which Jesus Christ is manifested anew to his people, in terms of both the promises which the gospel offers them and the demands which it lays upon them.

Let us grasp the nettle of our problem by turning to
the second form: the Word of God as Scripture. The
Word of God comes to us as something written, that is,
in the form of literature. This is the premise of all
biblical criticism, whatever the critical method: source
criticism, form criticism, tradition criticism, stylistic
criticism, redaction criticism, structuralism. To be sure,
some have advocated a hermeneutic that shifts the emphasis from the written Word to the oral Word. For
instance, Gerhard Ebeling, in his book *Word and Faith*
(pp. 428–429), declares that

> God's Word by its nature is not a written, once-upon-a-
> time word, but one that is orally spoken and happens. It
> is not the Bible text, but the proclamation, that is God's
> Word in the strict sense. Insofar as the proclamation is
> dependent on the text, the exposition therefore serves to-
> wards the text proving itself a Bible text, i.e., becoming the
> source of God's Word.

Ebeling seems to have blended Barth's three senses of
the Word of God into one, namely, the proclaimed
word—"the word that is orally spoken and happens."
Let us hope that such an event takes place in Christian
worship. We ministers surely know, however, that insofar as we engage in biblical preaching, the Word of God
does not come to *us* orally. It comes to us through a
chain of witnesses that leads across the centuries of
church history to Scripture: to what was written "once
upon a time" for us.

In this respect we stand on common ground with the
original Christian community. Early Christian preachers sought to understand and expound the marvelous
things that God had done through Jesus, the Christ, in
the light of Israelite traditions they had received in

written form. What they saw and heard was perceived "in accordance with the scriptures" *(kata tas graphas),* that is, the scriptures of Israel or, in Christian terms, the Old Testament. At the beginning of I Cor., ch. 15, Paul declares that the kerygma concerning the death, burial, and resurrection of Jesus, which he had received and had transmitted, was "in accordance with the scriptures." Moreover, Luke gives us a beautiful post-resurrection story about disciples who were walking along the road to Emmaus, bewildered about what had happened to their master (Luke, ch. 24). As they walked—so the story goes—they were joined by a stranger, unrecognized at first, who "opened their minds to understand the scriptures," specifically the Torah (Pentateuch), the Prophets, and the Psalms.

Admittedly, in the first century there was great un-certainty about the boundary of Scripture. Two of the parts of sacred literature referred to in the Emmaus story had already been completed and closed: the Torah and the Prophets. The Psalms, also mentioned in Luke's story, suggests a third part, the Writings, which in the first century of the Christian era was still in an open-ended, fluid state, with the result that there was room for rabbinical debate about marginal books (e.g., at the Council of Jamnia) or for including so-called deuterocanonical books in Christian theology and wor-ship. Nevertheless, uncertainty about the outer margin of the canon of Israel's Scriptures does not really affect the fundamental issue. Early Christians lived out of the Old Testament and they turned to this literature— Torah, Prophets, and Writings—to understand the things they had seen and heard concerning Jesus of Nazareth. Indeed, in the celebrated passage, II Tim. 3:16, the claim is made that "all scripture" is *theopneus-*

tos, or "God-breathed," an expression that recalls the
Yahwist's story of God breathing into the dust his life-
giving spirit so that it became a living being (Gen. 2:7).
It should be noted that the "sacred writings" which are
infused with divine vitality, according to the passage
from II Timothy, are the Scriptures of Israel (the Old
Testament).

Of course, today we understand that these three
parts of Scripture should not be regarded as fixed and
frozen blocks of literature; rather, they pulse with a
vitality that reflects a long history of traditions before
their final composition. As Gerhard von Rad and others have reminded us, "all scripture" must be regarded
not as on a flat surface, superficially, but in a "dimension of depth." Nevertheless, even when due regard is
given to this traditio-historical vitality, it remains true
that in the early Christian community the Old Testament functioned in the form of Scripture, as *literature;*
and in that form it has functioned in the history of the
church to the present. I am inclined to agree with Roland Murphy, who, in an essay on "The Old Testament
as Word of God" (in *A Light Unto My Path,* ed. by H.
N. Bream *et al.*), brings the accent down on the *written*
word. Although the phrase "word of God" implies "a
long journey through history," Father Murphy observes, it refers "in the first instance to the final written
word; it is with the Old Testament in its final form that
we are concerned." He goes on to say: "The reduction
to writing is motivated by the vision of the community
which sees in the word more than the immediate appli-
cation to a given generation" (p. 364).

Much of the debate over the written word—the
Word as Scripture—has dealt with the question of how
divine authorship and human authorship are inter-

related. Often the question has been formulated in terms of how the "letter" (Latin, *littera*) is related to the "spirit," that is, how the "literal sense" is related to the "spiritual sense" which expresses the divine intention. A key text in the debate has been II Cor. 3:6: "The letter killeth, but the Spirit quickeneth," that is, gives life, vitality. The traditional view is that God or the Holy Spirit is the "author" of Scripture. This came to mean that God is a "composer" in the usual sense of the English word "author"; and this must have been what George Adam Smith had in mind when he announced prematurely that modern criticism's war against traditional theories had been won. However, the word "author" is ambiguous, especially in its Latin form *(auctor)*. It may mean "originator," "instigator" (consider our expression "author of liberty"). In this larger sense we may understand the term when we say that God speaks through the medium of human words and that the Bible is "Word of God in words of man."

HISTORICAL CRITICISM AND SCRIPTURE

It is beyond my purpose and ability to trace the long history of the debate about the written Word—that is the province of a church historian. My concern at this point is immediate and practical: to understand the new and illuminating contribution that modern criticism— or, as it is usually called these days, "historical criticism"—has made to preaching. To bring the problem down from the clouds of debate into the area where ministers work from week to week, I propose to consider a specific text: the well-known story of the testing of Abraham found in Gen. 22:1–19.

It is appropriate to begin with the positive, especially in these days when historical criticism has become a whipping boy. The historical-critical method has taken seriously, though in its own way, the Pauline statement: "The letter kills, the Spirit gives life."

Historical criticism is concerned with the Word of God as literature, a term based on the Latin *littera* ("letter"). The question is: How do we understand this literature so that it ceases to be a dead letter, frozen in final form and useful mainly as proof texts for church doctrines, but instead becomes the living Word that is filled with liberating power? The historical critic answers: The Spirit endows the text with vitality by enabling us to go behind its final form and to inquire into its "historical sense," that is, its meaning and setting in the history of the people. The text that we have received has had a prehistory; it has been in movement, like a projectile in a trajectory. Therefore we can understand the vitality of the text by searching for its origin (original formulation) in its native life-situation *(Sitz im Leben)* and tracing its transmission through the generations, when it was appropriated and interpreted in new ways. Scripture (what is written) is not static, but dynamic; it is not to be read as on a flat surface but in a dimension of depth.

Consider what this dynamic approach means in the case of the story of the testing of Abraham. Historical criticism leads us through various stages along the way of the prehistory of the Torah that culminated in the final, received form of Scripture.

One stage is disclosed by analyzing the Pentateuch into component literary "sources" (J, E, D, P), each of which reflects a particular time in the history of the people. Among historical critics there is fairly general agreement that the Abraham story found in Gen., ch. 22, belongs to the Elohistic (E) source, which presumably was composed in northern Israel (Ephraim) during the period of the monarchy, possibly as early as the time of Elijah (ca. 850 B.C.). An excellent illustration of the evangelical possibilities of this source-critical approach is provided by Hans Walter Wolff in his essay on "The Elohistic Fragments in the Pentateuch" (in *The Vitality of Old Testament Traditions,* by H. W. Wolff and Walter Brueggemann). He maintains that the Elohistic document, though preserved only in fragmentary form, originally existed by itself. It had "its own technique of composition and an independent message," the most prominent theme of which was "the fear of God." The purpose of this document, Wolff declares, was to give a new interpretation of traditional materials of the "salvation history" for the period of syncretism following Elijah's career, when Israel "faced some of its greatest cultic, political, and social temptations."

The story of Abraham's testing, according to Wolff, is an admirable illustration of the Elohist's literary technique and concern for contemporary relevance. Here the narrator reinterprets the old material about the rescue of the son by showing how Abraham followed, step by step, the path of obedience. By a skillful play on words, the old expression *'Elōhîm yir'eh* ("God will provide") is transformed into *y^{e}rē' 'Elōhîm* ("fearer of God"), thereby highlighting the theme of "fearing God" also found in Gen., ch. 20, another Elohistic fragment. In short, the original intention of the story can be found by going behind the received text into the historical situation of the late ninth century B.C. The narrator's purpose, Wolff maintains, was "to lead the Israel of his day through the events in which

they were tempted" and to put them in a crisis of decision: obedience or disobedience.

This is truly an "evangelical hermeneutic," as Brueggemann characterizes Wolff's approach in the preface
to the book of essays referred to previously. It is appropriate to recall that Wolff was a member of the Confessing Church in Germany, which took a stand against
German Christians who compromised with the Nazi
regime. Clearly, this way of interpreting Scripture
speaks to the situation of faith. The difficulty, however,
is that the independent existence of an Elohistic document is the vulnerable point, like Achilles' heel, of the
Documentary Hypothesis. In the Anchor Bible Commentary on Genesis, E. A. Speiser assigns the story of
Abraham's testing to the Yahwist (J). Others have gone
further and have maintained that the very notion of an
Elohistic source is an error in Pentateuchal research.

Another stage of inquiry is advocated by form critics
who finesse the uncertainties of source criticism and
press further back into the prehistory of the Pentateuch. Following the lead of Hermann Gunkel, the
great pioneer of form criticism and history of traditions,
these critics trace the tradition back into the *preliterary*
period—before the J and E documents—to the time
when they arose, were shaped, and were handed down
in situations of oral performance. In this traditio-historical perspective the story of Abraham's testing has
several levels of meaning, something like the strata of
an archaeological *tell* (mound).

Let us start with the bottom layer of the mound. The
oldest level, if we follow the view of Martin Noth
(*History of Pentateuchal Traditions,* pp. 102–115), was
a pre-Israelite cult legend associated with a sacred place
whose location has been obscured in the course of trans-

mission. At this level, the tradition may have had nothing to do with the patriarchal figures of Abraham and Isaac but was an etiology (explanation) of the custom of commuting the sacrifice of the firstborn son by the substitution of an animal (cf. Ex. 34:20).

Superimposed on this stratum is another one. At some time in the preliterary stage Abraham became the central figure, and the story was reinterpreted in the light of other Abraham traditions in which the patriarch was present from the first. At this stage the story did not deal with the theme of numerous posterity (the theme of the divine speech in Gen. 22:16–18) but only with the succession from father to son—a succession that was threatened by the deity but at the last moment was permitted to continue. Noth suggests that Isaac may not have been the "son" at this stage. Be that as it may, the story underwent a special development in the circle of the Abraham people.

The historical critic uncovers a still higher level in the mound. Eventually, though still in the preliterary stage, the Abraham stories were incorporated into the patriarchal history, with its genealogical sequence of father, son, grandson (Abraham, Isaac, Jacob); and, above all, it was included along with other tradition complexes in the history of the promise. The narrative device for embracing the Abraham story within the larger whole is the special Yahweh speech at the conclusion (Gen. 22:16–18), which is introduced by the formula, "The angel of Yahweh called to Abraham a second time." In this expansion of the tradition, Yahweh promises Abraham that, because of his obedience, he will have a posterity as numerous as the stars in the sky and the grains of sand on the seashore, that his descendants will possess the land (i.e., "the gate of their enemies"), and that all nations will invoke blessing on themselves through Abraham and his posterity.

Finally, we reach the top levels represented by the literary sources: the Elohistic source (incorporated into the Yahwist to form the old Epic tradition of the patriarchs); the old Epic tradition, JE (governed by the theology of the Yahwist and incorporated into the Priestly tradition); and the Priestly work, which moves in a vast, architectonic plan from Creation to the Noachic covenant, from Noah to the Abrahamic covenant, and from Abraham to the cultic community constituted at Sinai.

Much more could, and should, be said about traditio-historical investigation into the "depth-dimension" of the text. But perhaps enough has been said to show that historical criticism endeavors to trace the long history behind the Word of God, from the earliest stages of oral performance through various stages of literary formulation to the final text that we have received. This kind of study can yield great gains for interpretation and specifically for preaching. For we come to sense that the text is not dead: it is pulsing with historical life. And this vitality becomes evident as we analyze the various levels of tradition, attempting to place each in a setting in the ongoing history of the people. In this process, the "literal sense" of the text becomes its "historical sense." From this perspective, the Spirit indeed gives life; the letter kills.

HISTORICAL CRITICISM AND BEYOND

So much for the positive. Let us turn now to the limitations of historical criticism and to a consideration of a new type of literary criticism that may do more justice to the accent on *sola scriptura* and may be more helpful for preaching.

The major weakness of historical criticism, in my judgment, is not that it is "historical" (concerned with history) or "critical" (faith seeking understanding), but that it tends to take us away from the text in its final form and fails to deal with the Word of God as Scripture, as literature. It leads us into excursions behind the text, into hypothetical areas of the text's origin and process of transmission, into reconstructions of the situations that gave rise to the original text or its subsequent reinterpretations—and it tends to leave us in that far country.

Let me sharpen up the problem by suggesting that you ask yourself how you would go about preaching from the story of Abraham's testing in Gen., ch. 22. Would you say that you are taking your text from the Elohist, though admitting to yourself (not to the congregation!) that the document is a reconstruction from fragments and, if it existed, may not actually reflect the historical situation of Elijah's time? Would you say that you are going back, via form criticism, into the preliterary stages and concentrating on one of the presumed layers of tradition? "Today I preach from the pre-Israelite layer of this story which has to do with the abolition of child sacrifice." You can see the problem that historical criticism gets us into. It is no wonder that many ministers turn away from the critical commentaries, in which the exegete is preoccupied with reconstructions of origins and the long process of transmission, to the so-called preachers' commentaries.

The time has come for the kind of literary criticism that calls on our poetic and artistic imagination, without sacrificing the insights that historical criticism has provided. Biblical criticism of this kind will start from Scripture, from what is written, from given literature. It will recognize and appreciate through historical criticism that the received text pulses with the vitality and dynamic of the Word of God over a long history. In order to understand the text we need to have ears sensitive enough to pick up the overtones from the past, for the final text is a choir of voices of various generations —some enriching, others perhaps dissonant. Such literary criticism, however, will recognize that these voices are composed into a whole greater than the sum of its parts. The final composition—the literature that arises out of tradition—transcends the original situations along the way of the text's prehistory and, as Scripture, has the power to speak to future ages. And because the Word of God *as Scripture* transcends the immediate hearers of an earlier generation, it may become Word of God for us who live in an entirely different situation.

Let us consider, then, the parameters of a literary criticism which is concerned with the Scripture of a community of faith, keeping the Abraham story before us. In this connection, I draw your attention to an essay by George W. Coats, "Abraham's Sacrifice of Faith" (*Interpretation,* 1973), which goes into the story in greater depth than can be done here. Notice that his "point of departure . . . is the received text, not a hypothetical reconstruction of earlier levels" (p. 390).

First, the task of the literary critic is to determine the appropriate literary unit (pericope) of Scripture and to delineate its own internal structure and dynamic. Is the unit marked by a clear-cut beginning and a rounded-off conclusion? Does it display an overall structure and design? What literary techniques are used to create impact (play on words, repetition, use of imagery, recurrent themes, etc.)? What are the climax points in the movement of the narrative or poem?

The story in Gen., ch. 22, provides excellent material for this kind of literary criticism. Here we have a story complete in itself, with a clear beginning and a definite conclusion. It is narrated with such literary effectiveness that the sensitive reader cannot stand at a distance, contemplating the narrative movement with bland objectivity or historical curiosity. In the first chapter of his book *Mimesis,* Erich Auerbach compares the dramatic literary quality of this story with a passage in Homer dealing with Odysseus' scar. Homeric poetry, he observes, is written with a certain flatness. Every detail is drawn in, the characters' emotions are clearly described, information is provided about time, place, and identity. The narrative is simple in structure, "uninvolved and uninvolving." The story of Abraham's testing, on the other hand, has a dimension of depth and mystery; it is "fraught with background." Instead of objective clarity, we find various levels of meaning, ambiguity about time and circumstance, lack of description of the thoughts and feelings of the actors. The story is told in such a way as to appeal to the imagination. It has a "gappy," open-ended quality, requiring that the reader fill in the gaps as he is drawn into the movement. The reader must go with Abraham step by step, coexperiencing his love for his only son, his bafflement about the strange command he was called to obey, and finally the moment of release when, just as the knife was upraised, his son was given back to him. Scripture in this case is word of imagination.

It is not enough, however, to appreciate the literary unit by itself. Second, we should consider that the unit

functions in a given scriptural setting—in the context of
the Torah story as we have received it. Therefore, it is
important to raise such questions as: How is the unit
related to what precedes and what follows, that is, the
larger narrative and theological context into which it
has been incorporated? How does the unit contribute to
the present literary setting—does it enrich the presentation? add a note of dissonance and mystery? introduce
unresolved theological tensions?

Again, Gen., ch. 22, is an excellent passage for this
kind of literary study. This story cannot, and should
not, be read in isolation, as though it could be detached
from its given narrative context. The story loses its
meaning if the reader does not know what is given in
the context, namely, that Isaac—Abraham's only son,
the child of his old age whom he loves dearly—is the
heir of the promise and therefore the only bridge from
past to future. Previously Abraham had burned his
bridges behind him by cutting his ties with his past in
Mesopotamia and going toward a future in a new land.
And now the only bridge into that future is about to be
destroyed! Does it not seem absurd that God who gives
the promise should take away the means for its fulfillment? Abraham was tested—tested as to whether his
faith was in the future or in the God who graciously
gives the future. As the concluding and climactic verses
of the story show (Yahweh's speech in vs. 16–18),
Abraham's testing functions in the history of the promise that binds the Abraham, Isaac, and Jacob traditions
together. And this history, in turn, belongs in the larger
sequence of God's covenants (Noachic, Abrahamic, Sinaitic) which, in the Priestly presentation that governs
the Torah in its final form, represents God's uncondi-
tional commitment of grace to humankind, to the

ancestors of Israel, and eventually to slaves whom he liberated from bondage and in whose midst he chose to tabernacle.

Let me repeat that we may gain some insight into this Abraham story by trying to recapture its original setting in life or subsequent settings in the history of tradition. Yet *we* do not hear the Word of God mediated through this story as members of an audience in the patriarchal period, or in the days of Elijah, or in the time of the exile. We read the story in its final scriptural form and setting—as *literature*. In this literary form it transcends its original boundaries of space and the particularities of time, calling upon readers of this and every age to become imaginatively involved in the narrative.

Third, the literary unit, taken in its scriptural or literary setting, should be read in the context of the community of faith—the believing and worshiping community. In part, this means that any scriptural unit or literary complex must be read in the context of the canon. The decision that certain writings are canon, that is, rule or norm for the faith and life of the community, was not an arbitrary decision made by formal vote in some council. Ecclesiastical bodies cannot make such far-reaching decisions unless they actually ratify what is already true in life and worship. In acknowledging the Scriptures of the Old and New Testaments to be canon, the community was only testifying that it found these writings to be the medium of God's relation to them and their relation to God.

But something more is involved. To interpret the Bible "contextually," as my theological colleague Daniel D. Migliore observes ("Scripture as Liberating Word," unpublished manuscript, pp. 19–21), means that "we go to Scripture guided by the faith and confessions of the church through the centuries"—confessions that are "reformable by Scripture" but that are nevertheless "hermeneutical guides." We read the Abraham story, then, in the context of the believing, worshiping community—a community that struggles to listen to and be obedient to God's Word in the midst of the world today. We read the story in its scriptural context of the history of God's promise and the testimony to his faithfulness, and from the text we hear this Word of God in *our* situation, not in some earlier historical situation that lies behind the final text. Once we are drawn imaginatively into the story, it becomes a portrayal of the testing of faith: the venture of the "knight of faith" (Kierkegaard's expression) into the realm of the absurd, into the "eclipse of God" (Buber) and the negation of his promise, the outcome of which —as a miracle of grace—is the gift of life and the opening, unexpectedly, of a path into the future.

CONCLUSION: INSPIRED TEXT AND READER

These are the parameters of the kind of literary criticism that takes seriously the Word of God as Scripture, as literature. Perhaps we need to wrestle anew with the question of the inspiration—the "God-breathed" character—of Scripture or, as one New Testament scholar (Peter Stuhlmacher) puts it, "the hermeneutical significance of the Third Article of the Apostles' Creed."

Emblazoned on my memory is a sentence from the late Abraham Heschel's book *Between God and Man.* He wrote (p. 243): "One must be inspired in order to understand inspiration." We should be able to understand that statement. We must, in a sense, be poets in order to understand poetry, dramatists in order to appreciate drama, musicians in order to enjoy music. So the Spirit must meet with our spirit for Scripture to become "God-breathed" or inspired. The Word of God, insofar as it is Scripture or literature, calls for genuine literary appreciation and the kind of involvement between text and reader that awakens poetic, literary imagination. God speaks to his people today through Scripture at the point of our imagination, that is, where the "inspired writing" meets the "inspired reader" and becomes Word of God.

Two

Word of Narration

Once again I turn to the book by George Adam Smith that I chanced upon last summer during a visit to Hay-on-Wye: his Lyman Beecher Lectures at Yale in 1899. In his second lecture, on "The Course and Character of Modern Criticism," Smith discussed the new horizons that were opened to view by historical and archaeological research. Back in those days biblical students were riding on the first wave of archaeological discovery. It was in 1853 that archaeologists, excavating at the site of ancient Nineveh just across the Tigris from present-day Mosul, uncovered the library of Ashurbanipal, the last great king of the Assyrian empire. Some years later the news exploded like a bomb heard around the world, when a young Assyriologist who had been deciphering the tablets in the British Museum announced the discovery of a Babylonian flood story and a Babylonian creation epic. The implications of this historical research proved to be revolutionary. For centuries the biblical past had been controlled by the dogmatic interests of the church. However, the divorce between biblical theology and dogmatic theology, which J. P. Gabler called for in his famous inaugural address in 1787, became a reality in the nineteenth and early twentieth centuries. The Bible was liberated from its ecclesiastical confines and was seen in the light of the history and culture of the ancient Near East. And since the Bible deals with ancient history, it was studied with a historical method.

Smith was concerned with how the new historical horizons affected the task of the preacher. How does one, for instance, regard the patriarchal history in Gen., chs. 12 to 50? He conceded that, "though impossible of proof," the stories of the ancestors of Israel "have at the heart of them historical elements," "a substratum of actual personal history."

> But who wants to be sure of more? Who needs to be sure of more? If there be a preacher who thinks that the priceless value of these narratives to his work depends on the belief that they are all literal history, let him hold that belief if he can, and confidently use them. Or if he cannot believe that Genesis is literal history, and yet thinks that it must needs be, in order to be used as God's Word, let him seek his texts elsewhere: his field is wide and inexhaustible. (*Modern Criticism and the Preaching of the Old Testament,* pp. 107–108)

In his elegant English, he continues: "Than these extremes there is, however, a nobler way." He then proceeds to urge that we give attention to the dramatic character of biblical narratives.

> To the sacred authors of these stories we cannot refuse a license of dramatic and ethical expansion which we, more consciously, permit in our own preaching. . . . As preachers, we cannot refuse to follow the narratives of Genesis [unless and until] we refuse to follow the parables of Jesus. . . . The power of the Patriarchal narratives on the heart,

the imagination, the faith of men can never die. (Pp. 108–109)

Late in the twentieth century the problem persists. Does the Bible present "literal history" or "imaginative story"? Can we say in the light of archaeology and historical research that "the Bible is really true," to recall the title of a book by Werner Keller *(Und die Bibel hat doch Recht)?* Alternatively, is the Bible only story—beautiful and engaging fiction with no essential relation to actual history? Or is there, as Smith suggests, "a nobler way" that lies between the Scylla and Charybdis of these extremes?

THE NARRATIVE MODE OF CHRISTIAN FAITH

It is appropriate to begin, as we did in the previous lecture when considering the Word of God as Scripture, with Christian worship. When we Christians gather together from Sunday to Sunday for worship, we participate in and reenact a story, in the context of which we acknowledge the identity of God and our identity as the people of God. Christian art, as portrayed in sculpture, murals, and stained-glass windows of cathedrals, bears witness to the involvement of all generations in the biblical story. The Sacrament of the Eucharist is, in some sense, a reenactment of the crucial event of the biblical drama. And preaching, if it is biblical preaching, aims to relate the congregation to "the old, old story," to refer to the title of a well-known gospel song.

Christian worship, insofar as it is a reenactment of the biblical story, is dependent on the theological and liturgical style that characterized the Christian community from the first. In his book *The Language of the Gospel,* the New Testament scholar Amos Wilder observes that "the narrative mode" was the distinguishing feature of the early Christian movement. Other religions and philosophies of the time emphasized eternal truths, ethical maxims, transcendental meditation, and so forth; but the Christian faith found expression in the telling and retelling of a story. "The narrative mode," Wilder writes, "is uniquely important to Christianity. . . . It is through the Christian story that God speaks, and all heaven and earth come into it. God is an active and purposeful God, and his action with and for men has a beginning, a middle, and an end like any good story. The life of a Christian is not like a dream shot through with visions and illuminations, but a pilgrimage, a race [i.e., a career or life course]—in short, a history. The new Christian speech inevitably took the form of a story." (Pp. 64f.) He goes on to say that this story does not allow us to stand at a distance, with academic detachment (like commentators who analyze the news or even professors who teach the New Testament!). For the story is not just about other people, but is also about us. We are involved, to use Wilder's language, "in the great story and plot of all time and space" and we are brought into relation with "the Great Dramatist . . . God himself."

The question that Scripture puts to us is: Where are *you* in the great story plot of all time and space? Where are *you* in relation to the great Dramatist? This "story" is authoritative, or canonical, not because of the testimony of Peter or Paul, or because of the decision of some early church council, but because it defines our identity as Christian people. It speaks to the fundamental issues of life: Who are we as a community? Who is the God who deals with us and with whom we deal? What is the life-style to which we are called as God's people? In a profound sense, the Christian story, which now comes to us in written form, is the script by which we live as a Christian community. The story is appropriately rendered into English by the word "gospel"—a word that goes back to Anglo-Saxon *gōdspel,* "good story," and came to be pronounced God-spel to suggest the meaning "God-story."

This "good story" or "God-story," however, is not confined to the script of the New Testament. The first Christians lived out of Israel's Scriptures (the Old Testament); indeed, as we have already seen, these writings were the only "canonical" Scripture they had. The early Christian community had *only* the Old Testament, and whenever the word "scripture" or "scriptures" was used, the term invariably referred to Israel's Scriptures. In this respect, early Christians were quite different from many modern Christians who consider *only* the New Testament, that is, the writings that were approved and "canonized" during the second century A.D. and later.

It may be that the time has come for Christians to identify with the early Christian community and to rediscover the Old Testament as part of "the story of our life," to use a chapter title from H. Richard Niebuhr's now-classic book, *The Meaning of Revelation.* As Niebuhr observed, the Christian penchant for confessing faith in narrative terms, rather than in abstract propositions or flights into mystical silence, is dependent on the testimony of the people of Israel, whose life story is related in the Old Testament. As Christians, we can hardly confess our faith in Jesus Christ apart from the narrative context of the Old Testament.

To be sure, the Christian possession of Israel's Scriptures (the Old Testament) raises a major question that has not been resolved to this very day. How are we to understand the coexistence of the Christian and Jewish communities, both of which share the same scriptural heritage, both of which are embraced within the electing and saving purpose of God, both of which belong to Israel, the people of God? Here we have a major theological conundrum! Paul wrestles with the problem agonizingly and valiantly in Rom., chs. 9 to 11; and in the end his thought rises to doxology as he contemplates in wonder and praise the amazing grace of God whose wisdom is unsearchable and whose ways are past finding out.

Despite the divine mystery of the coexistence of the two communities, Paul recognizes the fundamental significance of the Old Testament for *Christian* faith. In the same epistle (Rom. 15:4), quoting a passage from an imprecatory psalm (Ps. 69:9), he says that "whatever was written in former days was written for *our* instruction, that by steadfastness and by the encouragement of the scriptures [the Old Testament] we might have hope." And in I Cor., ch. 10, where he recalls episodes from the Torah story, such as the worship of the golden calf, he declares: "These things . . . were written down for *our* instruction upon whom the end of the ages has come" (I Cor. 10:11).

It is not proper to say that Christians tell a different story from that related in the Old Testament; rather, the Christian story is the final chapter of the story of Israel. In Christian perspective, the Old Testament is not about someone else—the Hebrew people of long ago. Rather, these things were written "for us"; they are "revelation" for us (contrary to Bultmann). The Scriptures of Israel are an essential part of "the story of our life"—a story that reaches its denouement in the life, death, and resurrection of Jesus Christ. Here it must be said again that this Old Testament part of the story makes a claim upon *us*, not because of decisions made by ecclesiastical leaders long ago in response to challenges from men like Marcion, not because of a treasury of proof texts that certify Jesus as the Christ, not because of a theory of the divine authorship of Scripture, but because this story defines our identity. Who are we as the people of God? Who is our God who lays his claim upon us? How is our calling to be manifest in a distinctive pattern of life? Without the Old Testament portion of "the great story plot of all time and space" we have only an incomplete understanding of who we are, who is our God, and what we are called to be and to do.

THE EXODUS STORY
AND THE IDENTITY OF THE PEOPLE OF GOD

So far we have used the term "story," perhaps as a concession to the current vogue of "theology as story"; but at times, almost in the same breath, we have used the word "history." In German the word *Geschichte* can mean either "story" or "history." In English, however, we have to make a distinction between the two words, and the distinction is fraught with theological significance. Does the Bible present history? or story? or a combination of both? The minister cannot escape these questions, as George Adam Smith pointed out years ago.

Let us bring the question down from the stratosphere of theological debate to the practical level where ministers face the task of preaching from Scripture in the modern world.

There is a sense in which all three parts of the canon of Hebrew Scripture are equally important: Torah, Prophets, and Writings. But if these three parts are equal, then—to recall a famous line from George Orwell's *Animal Farm*—one is "more equal" than the others. It is the Torah that is fundamental to the understanding of Israel's identity as the People of God. The word "Torah," as we well know, is inadequately translated as "law" (Greek, *nomos;* Latin, *lex*). To be sure, the Torah contains laws; but laws are set in the context of a story that extends from creation to the death of Moses in full view of the Promised Land. When the Torah story was brought from Babylonian exile to the struggling community in Palestine, it became authoritative or "canonical," not because Ezra had the support of the Persian government or because of the dogma of the Mosaic authorship of the Pentateuch, but because a dispirited people in Palestine found in the Torah the basis of their identity. Survival as a people was dependent on sharing and identifying with this story.

Within the Torah story, furthermore, not all parts are equal. The story unfolds in six movements: primeval history, patriarchal history, exodus story, Sinai tradition, sojourn in the wilderness, occupation of the land. Of these six "acts" in the great drama, two are crucial for Israel's understanding of its identity as a people and the identity of God Yahweh: Exodus and Sinai. These two movements represent the vital heart of the Torah story. The designation of these "episodes" as the heart of the Torah story is not an expression of scholarly preference. On the contrary, the whole Jewish tradition attests to the fundamental importance of Exodus and Sinai—twin episodes that deal with the themes of salvation and obligation, grace and demand, gospel and law. So deeply do they lie at the heart of the Torah tradition that even yet they are celebrated or reenacted in the Passover Seder. Emil Fackenheim describes them as "epoch-making events" or "root experiences," namely, "the saving experience" and "the commanding experience." The believing Jew, Fackenheim reminds us, "does not call to mind events that are dead and gone" —that is, ancient history that has purely archaeological interest; rather, "he reenacts those events as a present reality: only thus is he assured that the past saving God saves still, and that He will finally bring ultimate salvation" (*God's Presence in History*, p. 11). Memory becomes dramatic participation. So the traditional Passover Haggadah says:

> In every generation one must look upon himself as if he personally had come forth from Egypt. . . . For it was not alone our fathers whom the Holy One, blessed be He, redeemed, but also us whom he redeemed with them.

The classical exposition of the exodus story is found in Ex., chs. 1 to 15. The story begins amid gloomy scenes of oppression and humiliation; it concludes with hymnic songs of liberation and exaltation. In the beginning we hear inarticulate cries of distress from slaves who were victims of the mightiest emperor of the day; in the end, Miriam and her companions take the lead in praising Yahweh with singing and dancing:

> *Shîrû laYHWH   kî gā'ōh gā'āh*
> Sing to Yahweh,   for he is gloriously triumphant

The exodus story has its own integrity, like an act in a drama. Two things are noteworthy. First of all, like the story of the testing of Abraham (Gen., ch. 22) considered in the previous lecture, this is a "good story." The narrator tells the story so dramatically that the hearer is caught up in, and swept along with, the movement from oppression to liberation. Along the way there are many strange turns in the plot. Pharaoh, anxious about security on the Delta border, commands the destruction of all Hebrew male infants; but the Hebrew midwives interpret his edict quite liberally, and even Pharaoh's daughter is instrumental in preserving the future liberator. Also, Moses commits an act of civil disobedience (he murders an Egyptian taskmaster) and has to flee to another country; but even in self-imposed exile he cannot escape involvement in politics and finally returns to Egypt, where he confronts Pharaoh with the demand: "Let my people go!" Moreover, the narrator, by using a sequence of plagues, builds up suspense as Pharaoh again and again is on the verge of yielding, until finally the story reaches a peak of dramatic intensity: the break of slaves for freedom, Pharaoh's armies in hot pursuit, and the deliverance of fugitives at the sea just in the nick of time. In the end all the dramatic tensions of the story are relaxed in jubilant singing and dancing! It cannot be denied that this is wonderful storytelling.

But there is something more. Exodus, chs. 1 to 15, is not only a "good story"; it is a "God-story." Throughout the drama Yahweh is the main Actor and even the Director behind the scenes. Yahweh works in the background to save Moses, the future leader of Israel. Yahweh leads Moses, through a series of seemingly everyday occurrences, into exile from Egypt, into marriage to the daughter of a Midianite priest, and into the wilderness where, while tending the flocks of his father-in-law, he is drawn into God's plan against his own inclinations. Yahweh is the protagonist in the contest with Pharaoh, testing him so that he and the Egyptians might know who God is. And Yahweh intervenes at the critical moment in the story by driving back the waters of the sea so that the fugitive slaves can keep their tryst with him in the Sinaitic wilderness.

Clearly this is not "history" in the ordinary sense of the word. Johannes Pedersen, a Scandinavian scholar, maintains that we have here a Passover legend which gives "an exposition of the historical event that created the people." "The object," he says, "cannot have been to give a correct exposition of ordinary events but, on the contrary, to describe history on a higher plane, mythical exploits which make of the people a great people, nature subordinating itself to this purpose" (*Israel,* Vol. III–IV, p. 728). Whatever this "higher plane" may be, it is not the dimension in which the modern critical historian moves. No modern historian would presume to give a historical exposition by referring to "the acts of God." About the only time we encounter such language in the modern world is in insurance contracts or wills where "act of God" refers to some extraordinary happening, such as lightning striking a house.

So, here we have a "good story" and a "God-story," but are we dealing, in any sense, with history?

HISTORY AND STORY IN BIBLICAL THEOLOGY

If you have been keeping up with recent discussions of biblical theology, you have surely noticed that there has been a distinct shift from "history" to "story." The shift in emphasis is evident, for instance, in the writings of James Barr, my predecessor at Princeton Theological Seminary. In his 1962 inaugural address on "Revelation Through History in the Old Testament and in Modern Theology," he maintained that the concept of "history" is a modern "construct" which, at best, is suited to only a small portion of the biblical traditions and, at worst, leads us away from the literary form of the biblical texts. However, in his recent writings (e.g., his article "Revelation in History" in the Supplementary Volume to *The Interpreter's Dictionary of the Bible*), he proposes that a viable alternative to "history" is "story," for approximately one half of the Old Testament is narrative in character and is, at least, "history-like."

The shift from "history" to "story" has occurred during the last fifteen years or so, in the wake of the death of the so-called Biblical Theology movement which flourished in the United States in the period following World War II. A vigorous leader in the Biblical Theology movement was the late George Ernest Wright, a theologian who influenced me profoundly in my early teaching career and later became a theological friend and an archaeological colleague in the Drew-McCormick expedition to the site of ancient Shechem. Appropriately the posthumously published Festschrift to him was entitled *Magnalia Dei: The Mighty Acts of God* (1976), a title reminiscent of his *God Who Acts* (1952) and of an introduction to the whole Bible co-authored with Reginald Fuller, *The Book of the Acts of God* (1957). Speaking against those who wanted to treat biblical theology as a compendium of doctrines, Wright maintained that the God of the Bible is the God who acts historically, in real events and concrete circumstances which, at least in part, are open to historical investigation and which, in any case, are matters of theological concern. He firmly believed that his interest in archaeology, inherited from his teacher W. F. Albright, was not inconsistent with his theological concern, even though he was hard put to give a theological answer to the question which, according to Josh. 4:6, children ask of their parents: "What mean these stones?"

The Biblical Theology movement was shipwrecked on the shoals of "history." In an obituary for the death of the movement, entitled *Biblical Theology in Crisis* (1970), Brevard Childs observed that one of the major weaknesses was the emphasis on "the revelation of God in history." Contributing to the death knell were various scholarly works, of which I shall mention two in particular.

One was the brilliant *Old Testament Theology* by Gerhard von Rad, the first volume of which (dealing with Israel's historical traditions) appeared in German in 1957. In this work, the distinguished German theologian drew a sharp distinction between Israel's confessional picture of its own history and the picture of Israel's history presented by a modern critical historian (e.g., Martin Noth). Israel's picture of its history, he said, aimed for a maximum: it was a glorified version of a history of Yahweh's acts and of the people's response. The modern critical picture of history, on the other hand, reduces everything to a sober, prosaic historical minimum. Contrary to the claims of his critics, von Rad did not want to say that Israel's confessional history has no contact with actual, factual history. One gains the impression, however, that in his theological understanding facticity does not matter. Old Testament theology, he insisted, must be guided by Israel's *Nacherzählen,* that is, the telling and retelling of its history with Yahweh in ever-new situations during its ongoing historical pilgrimage. In this perspective, "history" is the history of traditions—the process of telling and retelling the Israelite story.

Another influential writing was an essay by Langdon Gilkey on the weighty subject "Cosmology, Ontology, and the Travail of Biblical Language" (*Journal of Religion,* 1961). I regard it as an honor to have been linked with G. Ernest Wright in Gilkey's penetrating criticism of the Biblical Theology movement of the time. In rereading the essay, after the death of various "instant theologies" of the '60s, I was impressed by two things. First, the essay was written in personal anguish. At the outset Gilkey states that he is personally disturbed, for he finds the biblical language about the acts of God in history congenial and, as a systematic theologian, uses the main categories of this language, but, he says, "I find myself confused about it when I ponder it critically." And second, he states with "honest-to-God" sincerity that we as modern people, who must live and think in the context of twentieth-century science and technology, simply cannot take a naive view of the biblical witness to God's acts and words. For the theologian it is one or the other: "You cannot have your cake and eat it too"—to quote a piece of modern wisdom!

You can see, then, that biblical theology has come a long way since the day when George Adam Smith gave his Lyman Beecher Lectures at Yale. The trajectory is a path from a positive, naive acceptance of the Bible as literal history through "the revelation of God in crucial historical events" to the present concern for "theology as story." The latter stage is illustrated by James Barr, who asks whether an event, in order to be revelatory, has to be an "outward" event and in that sense "historical." Cannot it also be, he asks, "a mental event, perhaps the perception of problems by a teacher or writer and thus a perception that starts a new train of thought and a new direction in biblical tradition"? ("Revelation in History," p. 746). He goes on to say that, basically, "the character of the Old Testament is story rather than history. . . . This narrative spirals back and forward across what we would call history, sometimes coming closer to it and sometimes going far away from it. . . . It is a cumulative story in which new elements are made meaningful through that which has gone before, while tensions in the existing tradition lead to changes and the formation of new tradition." The word "revelation," at least as usually understood, "does not fit with the structure of [divine] communication through cumulative tradition within the Bible" (pp. 748–749).

THE PROBLEM OF GOD'S PRESENCE IN HISTORY

Clearly the swing of the pendulum from "history" to "story" has theological implications that inevitably affect the task of preaching. It is not just "revelation in history" but "revelation" itself that has become problematic.

Developments in other scholarly disciplines have contributed to the moratorium on talking about divine revelation in history. Remember that during the '60s, when existentialism was in vogue and religious phenomenology issued in a "death of God" theology, the theological question was whether "God talk" is possible at all or whether all statements about God must be reduced to anthropological affirmations without remainder. In subsequent years biblical exegesis has come under the influence of modes of interpretation that are ahistorical or even nonhistorical. One influence, for instance, comes from the so-called New Literary Criticism that has commanded attention in the field of literature. According to this view, a literary work must be studied in its own right, without raising intrusive historical questions about authorship, provenance, original intention, and so forth. Once a literary work is completed, we are told, the "umbilical cord" that connects it with the author and his situation is cut, and the work leads a life of its own (J. P. Fokkelman, *Narrative Art in Genesis,* pp. 3f.). Freed from its original birth situation, the work appeals in its own narrative or poetic terms to the questions and concerns of readers far removed from the original circumstances of composition. In this connection, I am reminded of a passage recently brought to my attention in Northrop Frye (*A Natural Perspective,* p. 13), who tells the following tale:

> MADGE: Once upon a time, there was a king, or a duke, that had a fair daughter, the fairest that ever was, as white as snow and as red as blood; and once upon a

> time his daughter was stolen away; and he sent all his
> men to seek his daughter; and he sent so long, that
> he sent all his men out of his land.
> FROLIC: Who dressed his dinner, then?
> MADGE: Nay, either hear my tale or kiss my tail!
> FANTASTIC: Well said! On with your tale, granny!

The point seems to be that we should be so engrossed
with the story, so caught up in its word world, so involved in existential dialogue with it, that interrupting
historical questions are out of place. Whether the story
is based on anything that actually happened is irrele-
vant.

I do not wish to repeat the errors of the Biblical
Theology movement of a past generation; but there is
something theologically disturbing about this extreme
storytelling style of theology. The notion that the Bible
is *only* story, or that revelation (if we dare to use the
term) is only a mental event, sounds suspiciously like
a new kind of docetism. Students of theology will recall
that docetism is the view that God's historical revelation in Jesus Christ was only an "appearance," not a
historical reality. Translated into the context of the Old
Testament, the question is this: Did God really reveal
himself in an "outward event," the liberation of slaves
from Egyptian bondage, thereby providing a paradigm
of what he is doing in the world today? Or does the
exodus, and particularly the deliverance at the sea, belong only to an imaginative world of poetry and story?

Admittedly it is difficult for any of us who live and
think in the twentieth century to speak of God's presence in the world, whether in nature or in history. For
us, nature is not a sphere of God's activity, for we
belong to an age of technology, space ventures, and
computers wherein our understanding of the natural

world is governed by the presuppositions of the scientific method. And when we look around and behind us into history, and try to understand our past and present, we are also inescapably influenced by the presuppositions of a scientific method, commonly called the historical-critical method. In terms of this method, how can God be active in history?

The presuppositions of the historical-critical method were set forth with rigorous honesty by Ernst Troeltsch in his various works dealing with historicism—for instance, his 1913 essay entitled "Concerning Historical and Dogmatic Method in Theology" ("Über historische und dogmatische Methode in der Theologie," in *Gesammelte Schriften,* Bd. II). According to Troeltsch, historical (scientific) study of the past is based on three fundamental assumptions:

1. In the study of history we can arrive only at probability, not certainty.
2. Events of the past can be known only on the basis of analogy, that is, we can understand the unknown only on the basis of analogies known to us in our world of experience.
3. And, thirdly, historical events are related by a causal nexus, that is, in a chain of cause and effect.

It takes little effort to discover that each of these scientific principles presents a problem for biblical interpretation. The first principle (probability) seems to undercut the historical foundation of the community of faith, for how can we ever be certain about any event of the past, such as the crucial event of the exodus? The second principle (analogy) denies the possibility of our knowledge of a radically unique event, such as the resurrection, for which there is no analogy in observable phenomena of the ordinary world. And the third principle (causation) seems to deny the possibility of any direct action or intervention of God in history.

As modern persons, none of us can escape this challenge to faith. All of us, whether biblical theologians or systematic theologians, encounter the Bible from a standpoint that is given to us by modern history. About this matter Langdon Gilkey was refreshingly honest in his essay on ". . . the Travail of Biblical Language," mentioned above. In rereading his essay, I was struck by the fact that we can hardly escape the postulates of Troeltsch. Gilkey says, for instance, that "religious truth is universally available to all mankind, or at least [is] in continuity with experiences universally shared by all men." Immediately I am reminded of Troeltsch's principle of analogy, according to which any event of the past must be translatable into experiences generally shared by human beings if it is subject to empirical study and understanding. Also Gilkey refers to "the causal nexus in space and time," "the assumption of a causal order among phenomenal events," and hence "the authority of the scientific interpretation of observable events." And immediately I am reminded of Troeltsch's principle of causality. If we take this assumption seriously, Gilkey observes, "the majority of divine deeds in the biblical history of the Hebrew people become what we choose to call *symbols* [emphasis added], rather than plain old historical facts."

MIRACLE IN HISTORY

We find ourselves, then, in a situation comparable to that of George Adam Smith at the beginning of·the century, though perhaps one that provides more radical difficulties for theology and preaching. One way to face the situation, as suggested by Gilkey and other theologians, is to regard the divine deeds in history as "symbols" that belong to a world of poetry and storytelling. Another alternative, advocated by Gerhard Maier in his recent book, *The End of the Historical-Critical Method* (1977), is to reject Troeltsch and his whole household and to return to a pre-Gabler situation where dogmatic theology controlled the biblical past and related it to the present. In the former case, biblical preaching would be storytelling or poetry; in the latter case, as in Billy Graham's widely heard preaching, it would set forth doctrines supported by Scripture. The question is—as Smith asked long ago—whether there is "a nobler way."

It is my conviction that theologians should become more aware of the limitations of the historical-critical method in dealing with the subject matter of the Bible. This method, valuable as it is, does not provide an Archimedian point of leverage from which one can lift the whole world! The historical-critical method is itself historically conditioned, and therefore is relative in value. The method, with its various postulates, should not exert such a tyrannical sway that all dimensions of wonder and miracle are removed from life, and God himself is banished from human history.

A recent challenge to theology has been given by Emil Fackenheim, professor of philosophy at the University of Toronto, in his slender but weighty book, *God's Presence in History* (1970). This book, whose subtitle is *Jewish Affirmations and Philosophical Reflections,* was written in the shadow of the Jewish holocaust and thus treats the presence of God in the context of

radical evil that seems to argue for his absence.
Following an ancient Jewish midrash, Fackenheim begins with the testimony of Miriam and her companions—those original participants in the event at the sea when fugitives from Pharaoh's armies were delivered in the nick of time. In response to the sheer wonder of the event, Miriam and her friends took timbrels and led in singing and dancing (thus beginning the "liturgical" tradition that reached its climax in the hymns and thanksgivings of the Psalter). Fackenheim cites a midrashic account that contrasts the vision of Ezekiel ("wheels within wheels") with what the women perceived and celebrated. According to the midrash, Ezekiel saw visions and similes of God—or, as we might say, his experience was a "mental event" in the realm of poetry and symbolism. But "even the lowliest maidservant at the Red Sea saw what Isaiah, Ezekiel, and all the other prophets never saw." Fackenheim continues: "The midrash insists that not messengers, not angels, not intermediaries, but God himself acts in human history—and He was unmistakably present to a whole people at least once" (*God's Presence in History,* p. 4).

As a philosopher, Fackenheim reflects on this "root experience" of Jewish tradition: the presence of God in a saving event that a people experienced "at least once." "How can historical explanation," he asks, "come to an arbitrary halt in order to accept the Inexplicable—the presence of God? God, it seems, must be *expelled from history* [emphasis added] by the modern historian, just as He is expelled from nature by the modern scientist." Fackenheim goes on to say: "Neither modern Jews nor modern theologians can affirm God's real presence in history but, at most, only his providence over it." The result is that many people, in their search for God, engage in a religious flight from history "to an Eternity above history, to nature below it, or to an individualistic inwardness divorced from it" (p. 6).

This discourse on the "expulsion" of God from history and its consequences in religious life provides a penetrating critique of our modern world, whose presuppositions we take in with the very air we breathe. Notice, however, that Fackenheim does not advocate a retreat into either religious dogmatism about the past or storytelling fancy. Rather, he is impressed with the sense of wonder and miracle that lies at the basis of the tradition. It was a "root experience," an actual historical event, which inspired Miriam and her companions to break into song. Fackenheim quotes approvingly Martin Buber's discussion of the miracle at the sea:

> Miracle is not something "supernatural" or "superhistorical" but an incident, an event which can be fully included in the objective, scientific nexus of nature and history; the vital meaning of which, however, for the person to whom it occurs, destroys the security of the whole nexus of knowledge for him and explodes the fixity of the fields of experience named "Nature" and "History." . . . The real miracle means that in the astonishing experience of the event, the current system of cause and effect becomes, as it were, transparent and permits a glimpse of the sphere in which a sole Power, not restricted by any other, is at work. (*Moses,* pp. 75–77)

Perhaps this English needs translation! Let me try. There are rare, unique moments in the life of a people when an event occurs that explodes human rationalizations of "nature" and "history," even modern scientific postulates that are necessary for human understanding. Such moments evoke astonishment and wonder at the power of God, who is active in our world but who cannot be comprehended in any scientific scheme. Regardless of how the scriptural witness is understood, we must allow room in our thinking for the original "abiding astonishment" of the historical event, an astonishment whose reverberations are felt throughout the history of traditions as the story of the event is told and retold in ever-new situations of worship.

The theological problem presented by historical criticism is also addressed in a recent work by a New Testament scholar, Peter Stuhlmacher (*Historical Criticism and Theological Interpretation of Scripture,* 1977). This small paperback carries the tantalizing subtitle *Toward a Hermeneutics of Consent.* The English word "consent" may not be the best translation of the original German *Einverständnis* ("eine Hermeneutik des Einverständnisses mit den . . . Texten"). Stuhlmacher seems to mean that the text in its own way makes a claim to transcendence; that the exegete must be willing to listen and, as a member of the community of faith, to empathize and agree (consent). The initiative in the dialogue comes, not from the interpreter who imposes modern categories of understanding, but from the text which challenges our postulates of understanding. The method of historical criticism, he maintains, needs broadening in order "to allow room for the question of God and his activity" (p. 82), or, to phrase it otherwise, so that we can be open to transcendence. We find ourselves today in a position, he says, "where we have the possibility and freedom of making use of historical criticism where it is really productive, namely in historical analysis and description, and at the same time of transcending it where it threatens to restrict our encounter with historical reality" (p. 90).

STANDING ON HOLY GROUND

In summary, the problem that we have been wres-
tling with—the relationship between history and story
—should lead us to a chastened humility about our
historical study of Scripture. On the one hand, we have
no other ground on which to stand in our encounter
with Scripture than the ground of the modern world,
with its particular presuppositions and world view. On
the other hand, no one has been able to achieve the
ambition of Archimedes: to find an absolute point from
which to gain control over the universe. It is foolish,
therefore, to suppose that the modern historical-critical
method can expel God from history, even as it would
be rash to suppose that scientific method has banished
God from the realm of nature.

The corollary of humility in our historical study is
that we must allow room for a larger and deeper understanding of Scripture than is possible within the
categories of any one age, including our own. Perhaps this is what Barth meant when he reminded us
of the "freedom of Scripture" to challenge and reform our provisional understandings. For Scripture
brings us to an awareness of the mystery of God's
presence in history; and, as in the case of Moses, the
word addressed to any of us, wherever we are and
whenever we live, is: "Take off your shoes, for the
ground on which you are standing is holy ground."
Our historical study, our theological reflection, and
our preaching are grounded in "the abiding wonder"
of God's presence in our history. To this wonder the
entire Bible bears witness, not only in the testimony

of the Old Testament to the marvelous events that created Israel as God's people but also in the testimony of the New Testament to the re-creation of this people, and ultimately the whole of humankind, through the wonder of God's historical presence in the life, death, and resurrection of Jesus Christ.

Three

Word of
Liberation

These lectures have a kind of harmony, at least in the
assonance of their titles: word of *imagination,* word of
narration, word of *liberation.* Undoubtedly these for-
mulations betray a Hebraic fondness for the euphony of
words! It is my hope, however, that the harmony also
extends to the substance of our thought about the task
of preaching from the Bible in the modern world. In the
first lecture, you will recall, we considered Word of
God as Scripture—as literature—and the kind of literary criticism that is appropriate to the written Word. In
the second lecture we considered the Word of the Bible
in narrative mode: the story form of Scripture and the
problematic relation of story to history. Now we turn
to the central theme of Scripture: God's liberating
Word in human history.

As in the first two lectures, I take my cue from a
remarkable passage in George Adam Smith's Lyman
Beecher Lectures of 1899. He observed (*Modern Criticism and the Preaching of the Old Testament,* pp. 23ff.)
that "the Christian Church has twice over forgotten the
liberty wherewith Christ has made her free," and, on
the basis of a rigid interpretation of passages of Scripture, has imposed the harshest oppression upon people

through the centuries. Of course, he was concerned primarily with the Old Testament, but his strictures could have applied to the whole Bible. Under the conviction that the sword has been transferred to Christian magistrates, he observed, Scripture has been the warrant for "unspeakable cruelties" by Puritan ancestors, on both sides of the Atlantic, who "have not hesitated to defend their intolerance of opinions that differed from their own, their purchase and holding of slaves, their harshness to criminals, and their torture and murder of witches." There is some justification, he suggested, for the view that Scripture has been "a millstone around the neck of Christianity."

Here we encounter a remarkable paradox: the Scripture that should set people free has been an instrument for enslavement. The Scripture that should function as liberating Word has become, too often, a warrant for oppression. Thanks to liberating forces at work in the modern world, including historical criticism, many scriptural warrants of the past have been rejected. Surely no Christian theologian, at least in this country, is prepared to defend slavery or apartheid on the basis of Scripture. And in the Western world, witch-hunting has been transferred from the realm of the church to politics. There are other aspects of social life, however, where change may be retarded by a literal, rigid appeal to Scripture. One thing that comes to mind immediately is the "liberation" of women, a change taking place in the face of many scriptural passages, found in both the Old Testament and the New, which presuppose or even advocate women's subordination. There are also numerous other points of conflict with Scripture: the new sexual freedom in our permissive society, the rapidly increasing divorce rate, and—one of the most difficult problems of all—the emergence of homosexuals from their former anonymity. So we may ask: Is Scripture a "millstone around the neck of Christianity" in a time of rapid social change?

THE HISTORICAL CHARACTER OF REVELATION

Let us turn again to our central theme that the Bible is "Word of God in human words." In this theological cliché a whole biblical theology is epitomized!

Of course this is not the place to venture out into a full-scale theology of the Old Testament. If one were to tackle the task, however, the starting point would be a phenomenological understanding of the experience of the holy that Israel shared with other religions. Departing somewhat from Rudolf Otto's classical study *Das Heilige* (English translation, *The Idea of the Holy*), we would understand holiness, not just as a feeling of the mysterious and the numinous and certainly not as an idea, but as power that aggressively *breaks into* our human sphere, arousing both dread and fascination, as in the story of the burning bush (Ex. 3:1–6). The amazing proclamation of the Bible, found in both the Old and the New Testament, is that the aggressive power of the holy is not impersonal power *(mana)* but power that enters into our world with redemptive concern and ethical demand. According to the Torah's witness, the Holy God wills to have identity, to be God in relation to a people, to be accessible in prayer and worship—all of which is symbolized by the giving of God's personal name, Yahweh. The personalistic dimension of the holy, symbolized by God's personal name, is expressed in literary forms that expand beyond the declaration, "I am Yahweh," to the sentence form which encapsulates a story: "I am Yahweh, your God, who . . . ." Thus it is announced that Yahweh is the God who led his people out of Egyptian bondage, who led his people through the wilderness and into the Promised Land, who raised up adversaries to chastise his people, etc. Yahweh, the Holy One of Israel, is known in historical relationships, in the context of a human story.

The word "God," which is qualified by the personal name Yahweh, denotes neither the ineffable nor the familiar. To paraphrase Martin Buber (*Eclipse of God,* p. 51): If God were completely beyond the human ken, he could not be worshiped; and if he were totally immersed in history, that is, only a familiar phenomenon of our human world, he would not be worthy of worship. The amazing thing, to which Scripture bears witness, is that God, who does not belong to our world of thought and action, has chosen to become involved in our world: to speak through human language and to act through historical media. And if God has chosen to appear in our history, then historical study of Scripture is indispensable, for we are dealing with the Word of God in human words.

The historical study of Scripture involves a real, theological risk. We shall undoubtedly discover through critical study that the gulf between our thought world and the thought world of the Bible both widens and deepens. This risk, however, is related to the divine risk that God took in becoming involved with people like ourselves—people who are historical, finite human beings whose response to God's overture is conditioned by their situation in life, that is, where they *are*. And where people *are* in their response to God's revelation involves their sociological presuppositions, including their understanding of family, sex, war, and so forth. Christian theologians are surely right in seeing a connection between the risk involved in a historical study of the Bible and the risk that God took in becoming involved in human history—that is, the risk of the incarnation. In his essay on "Scripture as Liberating Word," my colleague Daniel Migliore speaks to the point:

> The Word became flesh. God allowed his Word to enter into the ambiguity and relativity of historical reality. The incarnation involved risk, and no doctrine of biblical authority is acceptable which denies or minimizes that risk. (P. 14)

The alternative, he insists, is a kind of docetism that refuses to take with radical seriousness God's penetration into our human world.

Thus God's revelation, or the inbreaking of the Holy into our world, is "historically conditioned." It would be a vast oversimplification, however, to suppose that the historically conditioned character of God's revelation is evident only in the Old Testament, as though the New Testament had special privilege. True, the Old Testament obviously reflects the sociological realities of its times: polygamy, concubinage, the right of the firstborn son, the limitation of priestly ordination to males, the apparent rejection of homosexuality. The problem, however, is not peculiar to the Old Testament. It is true that early Christians were radicals—eschatological radicals—who fervently believed that a new age was dawning and who criticized older practices, at least according to Matthew, as having been transcended: "It was said to them of old . . . but I say unto you . . . ." Nevertheless, the radical proclamation of the gospel

was inevitably conditioned by the sociological realities
of the time, including the institution of slavery (think
of Paul's letter to Philemon), the hostility toward the
Jewish community (remember Paul's discussion in
Rom., chs. 9 to 11), the subordination of women in
family relationships (see the tables of household duties:
Eph. 5:21 to 6:9; Col. 3:18 to 4:1), and the attitude
toward the state reflected in Rom. 13:1–7 (cf. I Peter
2:13–17). It is only by a highly selective reading of the
New Testament that the sociological problem can be
escaped.

Thus the "divine risk" must be taken with full seriousness. It is not that some parts of Scripture, which
seem to be more "spiritual," witness to the Word of
God (selected psalms, selected parts of prophecy, selected parts of the New Testament), as though a line
could be drawn between the divine and the human in
Scripture. Rather, the Word of God comes to us in and
through the historically conditioned writings of the Old
and New Testaments. God has taken the risk of becoming involved in the life of limited, finite, fallible, historical human beings, who respond to the divine action
where they are.

GOD'S SAVING ACTION

What, then, is the central theme of Scripture? The
answer to this question resounds against the sounding
board of Christian worship: the God whom we worship
has made known his saving purpose and power, preeminently through Jesus Christ, "for us and for our salvation"—to quote a phrase from the Nicene Creed. All
Scripture points to this one Center: to God, the Creator

and Redeemer, who wills and accomplishes human liberation from all powers of bondage.

In some circles it has been customary to say that Scripture sets forth a plan of salvation, that is, a *Heilsgeschichte,* or saving history, that proceeds according to a program that makes the whole Bible a unity. In recent decades biblical criticism has challenged this programmed view of Scripture, with the result that it is now easier to speak of the diversity of the Bible than about scriptural unity. In many ways the new awareness of the diversity of Scripture is a theological gain. Diversity helps us to understand that God wills pluralism and openness rather than narrowness and parochialism. Diversity enables us to speak of the richness of scriptural traditions, in which the contributions of various circles and many generations are brought together in the final whole. Diversity helps us to perceive more clearly the historical concreteness and sociological particularity of the "word" that expresses God's saving intention.

We should, however, resist the attempt to break the Bible into unrelated fragments, isolated circles of tradition, and antagonistic theologies. For in the midst of all diversities, Scripture witnesses to the one God, to his constancy and faithfulness, and to his zealous pursuit of justice and peace (welfare) throughout his creation. In this sense, both broader and deeper than any programmed view of salvation, Scripture bears witness to the saving intention and activity of God in human history. Salvation, in the theologically proper sense of the term, is the leitmotif of Scripture from beginning to end.

In the Christian community we respond with wonder and gratitude to God's saving action, to his "amazing grace," when we gather for worship. Those who attended the funeral service for George Thomas, held in Trinity Episcopal Church in Princeton (September 1977), received copies of John Newton's hymn "Amazing Grace." At one point in the service we sang the words that have been familiar to many generations:

> Amazing grace! How sweet the sound
> That saved a wretch like me!
> I once was lost, but now am found,
> Was blind, but now I see.

Indeed, this song found special meaning in the life of George Thomas, a philosopher of religion who sought to bring all thought into "captivity" to Christ, a pioneer in making religion a proper discipline of study in a university curriculum, and an active participant in Christian social action.

Particularly in the context of worship, there is something authentically Christian in this "eschatological" perspective. In a profound sense we are "citizens of heaven," as Paul said. We share the experience of being strangers and sojourners in a world that is not ours, something like the patriarchs of old, and hence we recognize that the true measure of life is not taken from our existence in this world. In short, we can identify with the Pauline "as if not" expressed in I Cor. 7:30–31: "Let those who rejoice rejoice as though they were not rejoicing, and those who buy as though they had no goods, and those who deal with the world as though they had no dealings with it. For the form of this world is passing away." The danger of this eschatological perspective, however, is that the experience of grace may be privatized, as in much popular piety. To be "lost" often means to be caught in the mundane world of politics and economics, and to be "saved" means to be translated into a new kind of existence in which one is related to a "higher world" or even to an otherworldly sphere. *This* world is accordingly devaluated, so that it is not the world of God's creation, not the sphere in which God has taken the risk of getting involved, not the context in which God's saving action elicits our response of action.

PARTICIPATING IN THE STORY OF GOD'S LIBERATION

So, Scripture in all its diversity bears witness to the God who faithfully pursues his justice, his *shalom* (peace, welfare) through history and throughout his whole creation. This is the dynamic theme of the biblical drama, in which we are invited to participate.

My esteemed friend and former colleague, the late Will Herberg, captured the spirit of biblical faith in a pregnant phrase of his own coinage: "faith enacted as history." This phrase is the title chosen for a recently published collection of his essays in biblical theology (*Faith Enacted as History,* ed. by B. W. Anderson, 1976). In the lead essay of that volume, entitled "Biblical Faith as *Heilsgeschichte:* The Meaning of Redemptive History in Human Existence," Herberg insists that the uniqueness of the biblical faith is "its radically historical character"—to the distress of philosophers and mystics who want to rise above history into a timeless realm, or of scientific naturalists who descend from history into nature, seeing man to be "nothing more than a biological organism adjusting to its environment." "Dehistoricizing biblical faith," he maintains, "is like paraphrasing poetry; something called an 'idea content' remains, but everything that gave power and significance to the original is gone."

The expression "faith enacted as history" is peculiarly appropriate to describe biblical faith. For the biblical "history" (Herberg could almost use the term "story") is a dramatic recital, indeed, a call to action with God. He cites the anecdote about an audience that is witnessing some tremendous drama being performed on a vast stage, when suddenly the chief actor steps forward, points his finger directly toward a person in the audience, and says: "You, you're wanted. Come up here. Take your part." None of us, says Herberg, are comfortable about this call—the voice of God that comes to us out of biblical history. As he says, "we much prefer the anonymity and irresponsibility of being spectators, and we resent the demand that we come forward, assume responsibility, and become actors." Nevertheless, the imperative to take part in God's history of liberation is inescapable—for those who have ears to hear.

In the Old Testament, the classic exposition of this fundamental scriptural theme is found at the beginning of the exodus story. The report of Moses' experience at the bush (Ex. 3:1–6) is supplemented by a divine address, whose function is to interpret what is going on in the story:

> Then Yahweh said: "I have seen the affliction of my people who are in Egypt, and have heard their cry because of their taskmasters; I know their sufferings, and I have come down to deliver them out of the hand of the Egyptians, and to bring them up out of that land to a good and broad land, a land flowing with milk and honey." (Ex. 3:7–8)

The story, which is told with consummate literary art, has two dimensions. On the one hand it reflects real events that were taking place in the empirical realm: slaves were suffering and crying out under oppression —victims of the mightiest emperor of the day. But although they were seemingly trapped in a no-exit situation, marvelously a way was opened for them to escape into freedom and to have a future.

There is another side to the story: not only was something marvelous and surprising taking place, but an invitation was given to take part in the drama of liberation. To Moses the invitation was extended: "Come, I will send you to Pharaoh, that you may bring forth my people, the children of Israel, out of Egypt" (Ex. 3:10). Negotiating with the stubborn Egyptian king was only part of the problem; Moses' task was also to convince an enslaved people, even against their inclinations, to want liberation and to move toward freedom. The narrator tells us that the slaves were too accustomed to their chains to want the risks of freedom. Right in the midst of the dramatic episode at the sea, when the slaves were on the verge of becoming free, they panicked and berated Moses:

> Is it because there are no graves in Egypt that you have taken us away to die in the wilderness? What have you done to us, in bringing us out of Egypt? Is not this what we said to you in Egypt, "Let us alone and let us serve the Egyptians"? For it would have been better for us to serve the Egyptians than to die in the wilderness. (Ex. 14:11–12)

Here is a story of human liberation (salvation) that portrays the dynamics of the oppressor and the oppressed. It sounds the theme that resounds elsewhere in Scripture; for instance, in the preaching of

Deuteronomy the people are told, "Yahweh brought us out" in order that he might "bring us in" (see the formulation in Deut. 6:23). Out of the old and into the new, out of bondage into freedom! Above all, the theme is picked up in the poetry of Second Isaiah, where the exodus is a "type" or paradigm of "the new exodus of salvation" that God has in store for his people. Exuberantly the prophet proclaims the surprising "new thing" that God is about to do in liberating a people from the external bondage of exile and the internal bondage of guilt and failure. And, of course, Second Isaiah's "good news" was finally picked up and transposed into a new key in the gospel of the New Testament which concerns liberation from all forms of bondage, outward and inward.

MODERN THEOLOGY OF LIBERATION

It is not surprising that in our time the biblical story of salvation has captured the imagination of people who suffer bondage and oppression and who find in the exodus story a paradigm of what God is doing in the world today through Jesus Christ.

In the United States the forerunners of "liberation theology" have been the members of the black community who, through song, preaching, and worship, have believed in God's liberating word, "Let my people go," even when the promise was long delayed. The liberating message of the Bible was the theme of Martin Luther King's preaching and leadership in the civil rights movement. And the good news of emancipation has been elaborated by other theologians, like James Cone, who find in the experience of oppressed black people a key for understanding what the Bible is all about.

Beyond our national boundaries there are stirrings in the Third World that are something like "the sound of marching in the tops of the balsam trees" (II Sam. 5:24) —a sign for David to bestir himself, "for then the Lord has gone out before you." A forceful spokesman of the new theological stirring is Gustavo Gutiérrez, whose book *A Theology of Liberation* has already gone into several printings. (See also José Miranda, *Marx and the Bible,* a book that also articulates the concern of the Third World for social justice.)

It is striking that Gutiérrez turns to the Old Testament, and particularly to the exodus story, in his exposition of the good news of God's saving (liberating) action. Salvation, he insists, does not involve a flight into a transhistorical realm or into an inner world of subjectivity; rather, God's liberation pertains to mundane social realities where suffering people are deprived of their full humanity. "The liberation of Israel," he writes, "is a political action. It is the breaking away from a situation of despoliation and misery and the beginning of the construction of a just and fraternal society. It is the suppression of disorder and the creation of a new order" (*A Theology of Liberation,* p. 155). Yahweh's action as Redeemer *(Gô'ēl)* of Israel, he goes on to say, is not just deliverance *from* bondage but, at the same time, deliverance *for* new life: "to bring them up out of that land to a good and broad land" and thus into a covenant community. He continues: "The Exodus is the long march towards the promised land in which Israel can establish a society free from misery and alienation. Throughout the whole process, the religious event is not set apart" (p. 157). Further: "With the Exodus a new age has struck for humanity: redemption from misery. If the Exodus had not taken place, marked as it was by the twofold sign of the overriding will of God and the free and conscious assent of men, the historical destiny of humanity would have followed another course" (p. 158).

Gutiérrez concludes by saying that "the memory of the Exodus pervades the pages of the Bible and inspires one to reread often the Old as well as the New Testament." For, he insists, "the work of Christ forms a part of this movement and brings it to completion and fulfillment." God's saving work in Jesus Christ is a new creation, in which "creation acquires its full meaning." It is wrong, then, to suppose that salvation through Christ is deliverance from sin in a purely individual sense. It is "at the same time liberation from all [sin's] consequences: despoliation, injustice, hatred." The gospel "fulfills in an unexpected way the promises of the prophets and creates a new people, which this time includes all humanity." Creation and salvation now have a Christological meaning, "for all things have been created in Christ, all things have been saved in him" (p. 158; cf. Col. 1:15–20).

These expositions of liberation theology provide excellent witness to the new and deeper understanding that may come through the historical study of the Bible. Scripture does not have to be "a millstone around the neck of Christianity," to recall George Adam Smith's phrase, but can lead us to realize in new ways "the liberty for which Christ has set us free." It bears witness to God's involvement in our history to pursue his justice and peace in the world. As we know from the witness of prophets like Amos and Isaiah, God displays a special concern for the helpless and the oppressed, those who are victims of the power structures of society.

Indeed, his saving work in history is like a two-edged sword: one edge is deliverance from pharaonic structures of power that tyrannize and oppress, and the other edge is liberation for a new life, for participation in a new community. To cite a theme from Mary's Magnificat, the God who is known through the biblical story humbles the proud and mighty and exalts those of low degree.

THE BIBLE AND OUR PARTIAL HISTORIES

Let us turn, now, to another dimension of the biblical story, one that is often ignored in attempts to translate God's liberating Word into modern history—or perhaps I should say, modern *histories*—in which various groups strive to realize their identity. The theological problem arises when "our story" is identified with "God's story."

Significantly, the story of Exodus and Sinai (deliverance and covenant relationship) is followed by the story of covenant-breaking (the golden calf) and covenant renewal in God's grace and forgiveness (Ex., chs. 32 to 34). To understand this narrative sequence, and particularly the episode of the making of the golden calf, let us consider a penetrating insight of Will Herberg in his essay on *Heilsgeschichte* to which I have alluded (*Faith Enacted as History,* ch. 1). Herberg observes that once we understand our existence in terms of history and examine "the [narrative] structure of our existence," we begin to see "that each of us has—or rather *is*—many partial histories, reflecting the many concerns and interests of life. We are Americans, members of a particular family, . . . intimately associated with particular social institutions and movements," and so on. He continues:

> Each of these concerns, allegiances, and associations has its own special history through which it is expressed and made explicit. But most of these histories, we ourselves realize, are merely partial histories; they define only fragments of our being and do not tell us who we "really" are. Underlying and including the partial histories of life, there must be some "total" history, in some way fundamental and comprehensive, some really ultimate history. Such a history, the history which one affirms in a total and ultimate manner, is one's *redemptive history, . . .* for it is the history in terms of which the final meaning of life is established and the self redeemed from the powers of meaninglessness and nonbeing. (P. 37)

In this essay Herberg anticipated what some of the "storytelling" theologians have been saying lately. Human existence has a basic "narrative" character. Thus "my story" or "our story" provides a significant point of contact with the Bible which also narrates a story or portrays a history.

Herberg, however, takes an important step beyond this. He quotes H. Richard Niebuhr (*The Meaning of Revelation,* p. 80): "To be a self is to have a god, and to have a god is to have a history." And, Herberg says, the statement could be reversed: "To have a history is to have a god; to have a god is to be a self." Thus, he observes, "if I take my American history to define not merely the American aspect of my life, but also the fullness and ultimacy of my being as a person, I make 'Americanism' . . . my faith and the nation my god." Moreover, the same can be said of Marxism which "takes the partial history defined by the proletarian status of the modern worker as the ultimate and 'total' history, and this history it proclaims as redemptive [history]." He concludes that idolatrous faiths "are faiths defined by, and defining, partial histories made ultimate." The partial history or story based on something in this world—some idea, institution, movement, power, or community—is lifted up and idolized; it ceases to point to the living God, the "God who is beyond the gods" of the world.

In this light we may be able to understand the sequel to the exodus story. The making of a golden calf is all too human! You remember the story: The liberated slaves became impatient about the absence of Moses their leader, and the absence of their liberating God who seemed to be so far off and transcendent. So they consulted a clergyman, the Rev. Mr. Aaron, saying, "Up, make us gods who shall go before us." Aaron went along with the people, though later on he tried to apologize for his involvement. Lamely he said that the people brought the gold they had collected to him and he "threw it into the fire, and there came out this calf!" Apparently the situation got out of his control.

The calf, or virile young bull, was a well-known cultic symbol in the ancient world, as we know from archaeology. The bovine symbol belonged to a story or a "partial history" that portrayed human involvement in the rhythms and cycles of fertility. The divine actors in the *mythos* or sacred story were Baal, the god of storm and fertility, and his female counterpart, Asherah, the mother goddess. This "story" was very tempting to Israel in an agricultural setting, as we know from prophets like Elijah, Hosea, and Jeremiah. The "sin" against which the prophets protested was that of taking something partial—some phenomenon in the world— and confusing it with the living God, the God who is

beyond all the "gods" of this world and their sacred
histories.

The sequel to the episode of the golden calf, as we
learn in the ensuing chapter in Exodus (ch. 33), is the
question as to whether Yahweh, the Holy One, can
really be with and go with a people of this sort—even
though it is his accompanying presence that makes
them distinct as a people and gives them identity and
vocation (Ex. 33:16). Moses, the covenant mediator,
intercedes for the people; and, in a special theophany to
Moses at the cave, Yahweh promises to forgive and to
restore the covenant relationship. Nevertheless, Yahweh's forgiveness is not "cheap grace." The identity of
God, made evident in the proclamation of Yahweh's
name (Ex. 34:6–7), is known to the people whom he has
liberated from bondage: Yahweh is the God who
abounds in faithfulness and loyalty, but does not ex-
empt from punishment. He is "slow to anger," but his
wrath (judgment) does not dissipate into indulgent love.

The dramatic account found in this part of the exodus story (Ex., chs. 32 to 34) is a profound exposé of
the human situation. Slaves, who had been emancipated
from bondage to oppressive social structures, all too
quickly fell into another form of bondage: they yielded
to the human temptation to identify something in the
world with God, their liberator. If I am not mistaken,
this is the burden of prophetic preaching in the eighth
century B.C. and later. Amos, for instance, perceived
that the story of God's liberation of a people from
bondage (Amos 2:9–10) was distorted into a claim of
special privilege. The God-story *(Heilsgeschichte)* was
identified with the people's story—and hence with the
values and life-style of a nation. Amos almost went so

far as to scrap the sacred story, the *Heilsgeschichte,* saying that the God who brought Israel out of Egypt also brought the Philistines from Caphtor and the Syrians from Kir (Amos 9:7). Forget the sacred story, he said, if it becomes identical with, and a justification for, the life-style of a people!

Similarly, Hosea perceived that the people whose identity was given them in the exodus story (Hos. 13: 4–6) had turned to another "story" which promised them the blessings of fertility and an economic boom. The "forgetting" of Yahweh who brought his people out of the land of Egypt, about which we hear so much in the preaching of Hosea and Jeremiah (also in Deuteronomy), was not ordinary amnesia, like a professor's absentmindedness. Rather, this was a forgetfulness rooted in the *will*—in the eager and passionate pursuit of "worldly" gods and their sacred histories. According to prophets like Hosea and Jeremiah, the bondage of the will was so imprisoning, the hardness of the heart so impenetrable, the deceitfulness of the mind so subtle (cf. Jer. 17:9) that only the severest "shock treatment" in the form of historical catastrophe could bring the people to their senses and restore their memory of the God who liberated them from pharaonic bondage.

How easy it is for us to identify our "partial histories" with the history of God or the God-story! No wonder that Paul, with real theological and homiletical insight, turned to the stories about Israel in the wilderness, including the episode of the golden calf (I Cor., ch. 10). He says that these things resulted in warnings for Israel, but "they were written down *for our instruction,* " that is, for us Christians, "upon whom the end of the ages has come." Therefore, he concludes, "let anyone who thinks that he stands take heed lest he fall!" (I Cor. 10:11–12).

THE STRANGENESS OF THE BIBLICAL STORY

If we are honest in our exposition of Scripture and honest about how Scripture interprets us, we are driven to the conclusion that there is something very strange about the biblical story—something that we cannot reduce to the categories of our experience, something that cannot be domesticated within our world. There is a "scandalous," offensive dimension to the biblical story. For the story of God's saving action, of his pursuit of justice and reconciliation, cannot be reduced to, or fully grasped within, the social situation in which people tell and retell the God-story.

Thus the biblical story of God's liberating activity provides both support for and criticism of liberation movements—that is, our "partial histories." Clearly some of these partial histories help us to perceive dimensions of the scriptural story more clearly. I would say that this is especially true in regard to the new perspectives opened up by black theology, by the women's liberation movement, and by the theological ferment of the Third World. These movements have helped us to rediscover the biblical story. At the risk of sounding impertinent, however, I must add that we should be on guard against supposing that "our story," whatever it is, is identical with God's story. There is something alien about the biblical story which challenges us, intrigues us, judges us, and perhaps brings us to the worshipful posture of Moses after the proclamation of Yahweh's name (Ex. 34:8). To hear the word of God's forgiveness, as in this part of the exodus story, should elicit the response of "fear" (reverence) of God (cf. Ps. 130:4), whose thoughts are not our thoughts, and whose ways transcend our ways.

It may be that some of the theologies of our time, even those which take seriously the narrative (story) structure of our existence, need to grapple more seriously with the alien dimension of the biblical story. Here I am influenced by my colleague Daniel Migliore, a systematic theologian who insists that the biblical story is "both an authorization and a continuing criticism of our liberation movements." "For every liberation movement," he writes, "insofar as it appeals to God at all, tends to identify God with a particular group. But the God of the biblical story, whose way of liberation is self-giving love, is always greater than what we imagine or wish divinity to be" ("Scripture as Liberating Word," pp. 18–19). We must be on guard, then, lest we so "privatize" Scripture that God's story is identified with "my story"; and likewise we must avoid the peril of ideology, that is, the equation of the God-story with "our story"—with the values and aspirations of a particular group, nation, or social movement. As Paul reminds us in I Cor., ch. 10, the story of the golden calf was written *for us;* for we Christians should beware lest we succumb to the temptation of identifying our partial histories with the story of God's redemption.

If we are to transcend our partial histories so that God's story can exert the power to reshape our identity, then I believe the historical study of Scripture is our indispensable ally. The historical-critical study of Scripture helps us to understand the strangeness of the biblical story: its pastness, its distance from our imme-

diate situation, its rootage in concrete experiences of
people of long ago. Of course, this story is addressed to
us, wherever we are in our particular life stories or
partial histories. It calls us to a "faith enacted as history," to responsible participation in God's story of
liberation. But the story has the power to reshape our
identities and to redirect our lives only because, in the
first instance, it witnesses to God's story of involvement
in our history, and only inasmuch as it makes us aware
of God's identity, God's faithfulness, God's judgment
and mercy.

IMPROVISING ON THE STORY PLOT OF SCRIPTURE

Though it may sound paradoxical, there is a sense in
which God's liberating Word liberates us from Scripture—at least from bondage to Scripture, so that we
may hear and respond to the Word of God anew in our
time. We belong to a community that is called to be
obedient to God's Word now, to respond to the scriptural story in the struggles of our world. And this vocation calls for "improvisation" in the freedom that the
Holy Spirit gives us.

At one of our luncheon conversations, Will Herberg
called my attention to the *commedia dell'arte,* or im-
provisational comedy, which flourished in seventeenth-
and eighteenth-century Italy. The players were asked to
improvise. To be sure, it was not a free improvisation,
for there were some given elements. There was, first, the
director of the dramatic group; second, there was a
company of actors bound together in relationship; and
third, there was a story plot—a script—that was given
them in broad outline. With these given elements—the

director, the company of actors, the story plot—they were told to improvise.

That is a fairly good analogy for understanding our vocation as ministers, whose task is to interpret the good news to the modern world. There are the same given factors. First, we should know that we are under the One Director or, as Amos Wilder put it, "the Great Dramatist, God himself." Second, we are part of a company of actors: the immediate Christian community and the larger "communion of the saints"—that is, the church with its tradition and its confessions of faith. And finally, we are given a script, the Scripture that presents the story plot. With these given factors, we are called to improvise on the script, to tell and retell the old story which has the power to shape and direct human lives and human society. But always we should know that our improvisations—our translations into our partial histories—are incomplete and inadequate. They cannot be identified with the great story, the meta-story to which Scripture bears witness: namely, the story of God, who has chosen to involve himself in our human history.

Four

Word of Obligation

BIBLICAL FAITH AND POLITICAL RESPONSIBILITY

Throughout the twentieth century, and well before, American religion has been polarized into what one church historian has called a "Two-Party System" (Martin Marty, *Righteous Empire,* especially ch. 17). One party, "the largely silent majority," emphasizes salvation from the political structures in which we live and move and have our being. According to this view, the Christian gospel may have a beneficial influence upon society, but the primary concern is the salvation of the individual soul which results in a piety and morality consonant with, and preparatory to, otherworldly fulfillment. Leaders like Dwight L. Moody and Billy Graham are spokesmen of this powerful party. The other party does not eliminate the otherworldly horizon but stresses social Christianity, that is, the responsibility of the believing community to act within the judgment and grace of God to transform the social structures which impoverish human life and deny any meaningful fulfillment in this world. Walter Rauschenbusch and Reinhold Niebuhr are leading representatives of this party movement.

All of us can easily find evidences of this two-party strife in the life of the church. Let me cite two illustrations from our recent history. The first takes us back to the height of the war in Vietnam. The Paris peace negotiations had broken down, and a presidential command was given to bomb North Vietnam. Indeed, in late 1972 we were even counting the bombing days left until Christmas! In that period, when churchmen were called upon to advise how Christians should respond, Billy Graham, in response to various inquiries, issued "A Clarification." "I am convinced," he wrote, "that God has called me to be a New Testament evangelist, not an Old Testament prophet! While some may interpret an evangelist to be primarily a social reformer or political activist, I do not! An evangelist is a proclaimer of the message of God's love and grace in Jesus Christ and the necessity of repentance and faith. My primary goal is to proclaim the Good News of the Gospel of Jesus Christ. The basic problem of man is within his own heart" (*Christianity Today,* 1972–1973). The second illustration also goes back to that crisis period, when the late Jewish philosopher, Abraham Heschel, was interviewed by Carl Stern on an NBC television program. The interviewer recalled that at the Berrigan trial prospective jurors said to the judge, one after the other, that they thought it was wrong for ministers to get mixed up in politics, for their job was to minister to spiritual needs. Heschel quickly replied that if the prophets of ancient Israel were alive today, those jurors would surely send them to jail. "And frankly," he added with a wry smile, "I would say that God seems to be a nonreligious person," for "he always mixes in politics and social issues" ("A Conversation with Dr. Abraham Joshua Heschel," Feb. 4, 1973).

In the dispute between individual and social religion, both parties claim that the Bible is on their side. In a sense this is true, although each appeals to *parts* of the canonical whole. My thesis is this: although the "two-party" division has been encouraged by the peculiar dynamics of American history, the conflict is rooted in the Bible itself where two religious perspectives, the prophetic and the apocalyptic, are joined in creative tension. Since the Old Testament is dominated by the prophetic view and the New Testament is heavily influenced by the apocalyptic perspective, the problem, in the last analysis, is that of understanding the interrelationship of the two Testaments.

The Political Mold of Biblical Theology

Before we turn our attention to these two perspectives, the prophetic and the apocalyptic, it is necessary to say something about the historical concerns and conceptuality that underlie both. At a recent Princeton Theological Seminary faculty seminar, my colleague George Hendry, a systematic theologian, introduced a fundamental thesis in an essay on "The Theology of Nature." "Biblical theology," he said, "is cast in a political mold: it focuses on the relation between God and the historical life of Man in society, and its conceptuality is predominantly political" (unpublished manuscript, Jan. 17, 1974).

It is difficult to contest the validity of this statement, although various efforts are being made in our time to challenge and correct a one-sided emphasis on "revelation in history"—for example, the famous essay by Lynn White ("The Historical Roots of Our Ecologic

Crisis," *Science,* 1967) which traces the roots of the ecological crisis to the Jewish-Christian motif of "the image of God" (see also my essay "Human Dominion Over Nature," in *Biblical Studies in Contemporary Thought,* ed. by Miriam Ward). The Bible, especially in its doctrine of creation, has much to say about the display of God's glory in heaven and earth and about the interrelation of "nature" and "history" in the drama of redemption. Nevertheless, Hendry rightly emphasizes that the conceptuality of the Bible—and this holds true for both prophetic and apocalyptic perspectives—is "predominantly political." This view is also maintained by Eric Voegelin, one of the leading political philosophers of our time. Ancient Israel, he points out, broke with the ancient Near Eastern pattern of symbolization, one which expressed mythically the integration of society into the divine being which orders the cosmos, and, through the agency of Moses, became a society living in immediacy under the Kingship of Yahweh. This breakthrough into "transcendence" was revolutionary, and the consequence was that there appeared "a new type of man on the world-political scene" (*Israel and Revelation;* see also my essay "Politics and the Transcendent," in *Eric Voegelin's Search for Order in History,* ed. by Stephen McKnight).

The fundamental witness to this revolution (or revelation!) is the Torah story, which is the inner substance of the canon of the Hebrew Bible and around which, as it were, the other canonical units (Prophets and Writings) are arranged concentrically. The heart of the classical Israelite story, which in Christian conviction is also part of the whole biblical story, is the dramatic portrayal of the inbreaking of divine holiness as redemptive concern and ethical demand. At a time when a hopeless and helpless band of slaves was victim of the mighty Pharaoh of Egypt, the Holy One (whose name is Yahweh) became involved in their plight and gave them a future. A political event—the liberation of slaves from bondage—was "the root experience," as Emil Fackenheim terms it, and also became the root metaphor for the people's understanding of its identity and the identity of the God to whom they were related. The corollary of this "saving experience," Fackenheim points out, was the "demanding experience," that is, the call to coexistence with God in covenant relationship (*God's Presence in History,* especially ch. 1). Thus the announcement, "I am Yahweh your God, who brought you out of the land of Egypt" (Ex. 20:2) has its sequel in the covenant pledge, "All that Yahweh has spoken we will do, and we will be obedient" (Ex. 24:7).

It is noteworthy that the symbolization of the Israelite story, based on "root experiences," is drawn from the field of politics. This is true not only of the exodus of slaves from political bondage but also of the covenant. Thanks to recent studies, especially those of Delbert Hillers and Dennis J. McCarthy, we know that *berîth,* which means "covenant" or "treaty," belongs to the language of ancient international politics. In some circles, represented notably by the book of Deuteronomy, a major treaty form, the so-called suzerainty covenant, was adopted as a model for understanding the relation between God and people. Basically, Israel's theological understanding was cast in a "political mold." It is true that Israel also appropriated motifs from ancient mythology, such as the conflict of the Divine Warrior with the Sea (waters of chaos) or even the sacred marriage, in order to enrich and elaborate the story told in faith. But the basic images—the root metaphors—were not taken from mythology, but rather from the sphere of politics: liberation from bondage, the covenant, divine suzerainty, the Kingdom of God, the City of God. In other words, models for theological understanding were not drawn from natural processes which were understood in sexual terms (the loves and wars of the gods and goddesses) but from historical experiences that illuminated the relation between God and man in society. Even the sexual motif of the sacred marriage, when boldly used by Hosea, was politicized to refer to the historical relationship between God and people.

From the very first, however, the theological problem was how to affirm God's activity in the "political" sphere, which is the native sphere of our human existence, in the face of opposing powers which limit or threaten the *shālôm* (peace, well-being) which the covenant was intended to realize, not only for Israel but ultimately for the nations as well, as portrayed in the well-known vision of the "last days" in Isa. 2:2–4. What is the nature of the "evil" which frustrates or threatens the realization of God's purpose in society? It is not accidental that the Torah story, in its present form, supplements the vision of the order and harmony of God's Creation (Gen. 1:1 to 2:3) with the story of "paradise lost," which deals with the flaw that leads to disorder and disharmony. The test of any religion or philosophy is how it deals with the problem of evil; and Israel was subjected to that test preeminently because of the fundamental affirmation of faith that God is involved in the Israelite story, as in the whole human story.

PROPHECY AND POLITICS

The literature of the Prophets presents a new perspective on the "root experiences" enshrined in the Torah. The task of Israel's prophets was to interpret the Israelite story in times when the monarchy was threatened and dominated by a succession of foreign empires: Assyria, Babylonia, Persia. Although the prophets spoke with different accents, they shared the central conviction that Yahweh was actively involved in the historical arena to accomplish his purpose. As in the case of the Egyptian Pharaoh at the time of the exodus, political powers—whether a foe from the north or from the south—were operating within the purpose of God to accomplish what Isaiah called a "strange work" (Isa. 28:21).

The father of the sociology of religion, Max Weber, began his study of "charismatic" prophecy with a discussion of "political orientations of preexilic prophecy." He described the prophets as demagogues in the best sense of the word—that is, leaders of the people whose predominant concern was "the destiny of the state and the people" (*Ancient Judaism,* especially pp. 267ff.). This observation remains true, despite subsequent changes in scholarly views. From the moment prophecy appeared on the Israelite scene it was intimately connected with politics. Tradition portrays Samuel, the first great Israelite prophet, as a successor to the charismatic judges of the Tribal Confederacy. He appeared in a transitional time, when it was necessary to reconcile the new political institution of kingship with the theocratic traditions of the old tribal order.

The prophet was, as G. Ernest Wright put it, the charismatic agent in "the politics of God," that is, the divine government which upheld justice in Israel and the surrounding nations ("The Nations in Hebrew Prophecy," in *Encounter,* 1965). Accordingly, they sometimes thought of themselves as having received their commission in the heavenly council. Jeremiah said of the popular prophets, who pandered to nationalism, that they failed to understand the political situation in a dimension of transcendence; "for who among them has stood in the [heavenly] council of Yahweh, to perceive and to hear his word, or who has given heed to his word and listened?" (Jer. 23:18). Yahweh's prophets were drawn into his cosmic administration, so to speak, and it was their task to translate the heavenly vision into the realm of pragmatic politics, even though they were not practical politicians. Jeremiah, according to the account of his call, was commissioned to be "a prophet to the nations" and, in speaking on behalf of God, to exercise authority "over nations and over kingdoms" (Jer. 1:5, 10). In some sense, the prophets were called to a "political office."

In their interpretation of the sufferings and disasters of the Israelite people, the prophets display an amazing consensus, despite their differences from one another. They do not portray human beings as victims of demonic forces or a power of fate; rather, they consistently take the people to task for a failure to exercise their God-given responsibility. Israel had failed to do justice *(mishpāṭ),* to practice *ḥesed* (loyalty), and to walk humbly with God (cf. Micah 6:8). The nations round about had violated Yahweh's international law, as Amos declared; but more specifically, Israel had violated the covenant law which is summed up succinctly in the Decalogue. In season and out, the prophets called for repentance, that is, a change of the life-style of the whole people, a life-style so perverse that even the land and the sphere of "nature" had been polluted (cf. Hos. 4:1–3; Jer. 3:2–3). If in the face of the political crises and the repeated appeals of Yahweh's messengers the people refused to change—to abandon false idols and to redirect their will to the true Source of their existence —disaster was inevitable, and they had no one to blame but themselves. "Your ways and your doings have brought this upon you," Jeremiah proclaimed. "This is your doom [*ra'ah,* "evil, disaster"], and it is bitter; it has reached your very heart" (Jer. 4:18).

The prophets were unbending in their insistence upon human responsibility. In a monolithic fashion, they interpreted Israel's sufferings in the political arena as *deserved punishment.* To be sure, they did not attempt to smooth out the paradox of divine sovereignty and human freedom. In one sense, they insisted, the judgment manifest in historical events would be the fruit of the people's ways—their misplaced priorities and their false life-style; "for they sow the wind, and they shall reap the whirlwind" (Hos. 8:7). In another sense, however, the judgment would be God's punitive action, accomplished through world powers operating within his cosmic rule. In the eighth century B.C., Isaiah of Jerusalem declared that the Assyrian dictator was "the rod of Yahweh's anger" (Isa. 10:4–19) by which he was accomplishing his *opus alienum.* In a similar vein, Jeremiah declared a century later that Nebuchadnezzar, the Babylonian ruler, was the "servant" of Yahweh (Jer. 43:10). Still later, Second Isaiah hailed Cyrus of Persia as Yahweh's "messiah" or anointed (Isa. 45:1). The prophets, however, sensed the arrogance of world powers and insisted that, in the final analysis, they too would come under divine judgment. As Isaiah said, the ax cannot boast against the one who wields it (Isa. 10:12–19); and Jeremiah declared that the world powers would have to drink "the cup of the wine of divine wrath" (Jer. 25:15–29). For the time being, however, God was working through political realities to accomplish his purpose.

The prophets who proclaimed God's judgment upon Israel and the nations were prophets of hope for this world. Indeed, they shifted the emphasis from the tradition of the past, which was reaffirmed or contemporized in the cult (see Deut. 5:2–3!), to the announcement of God's *advent,* his coming toward them from the future. Amos summoned the people to prepare to meet their God (Amos 4:12). According to Jeremiah, Yahweh was destroying the old structures in order to build and plant anew (Jer. 1:10; 45:1–5). And Second Isaiah could exhort the people not to remember "the former things," for Yahweh was going to create something radically new which would outshine any events of the past (Isa. 43:18–19; compare, however, ch. 43:8–9) (see my essays on Second Isaiah in *Israel's Prophetic Heritage* and in *Magnalia Dei: The Mighty Acts of God,* ed. by F. M. Cross *et al.*). The prophetic *Novum,* however, was not to be realized in a distant consummation or a transfiguration of history: it was to occur under the conditions of historical existence. While the prophets had no political program, they perceived that at the depths of the political crises of their day God was at work and indeed was compassionately involved leading his people to a new beginning. The continuity into the future was symbolized by Jeremiah's purchase of a field, his family estate in Anathoth, which, during the final siege of

Jerusalem, lay in enemy territory. The opportunity to buy the tract of land while he was in prison, under suspicion of treason, was to him a sign of the creative possibilities that Yahweh was going to open up in the immediate future: "Fields shall be bought in this land of which you are saying, It is a desolation, without man or beast" (Jer. 32:43).

THE APOCALYPTIC PERSPECTIVE

Let us turn now to the apocalyptic perspective. Literature of this kind is found on the margin of the prophetic corpus as a reinterpretation of classical prophecy —for instance, Isa., chs. 24 to 27 ("the little apocalypse") and Zech., chs. 9 to 14 ("Deutero-Zechariah"). As a distinctive literary genre, apocalyptic is exemplified in the Book of Daniel, which was included in the third, open-ended division of the Hebrew Bible, known as the Writings or Hagiographa. Significantly, the apocalypse of Daniel, which is popularly thought to be a parade example of prophecy, is not included in the canon of the Prophets in the Hebrew Bible. Indeed, the differences between the prophetic and the apocalyptic perspectives are so profound that some scholars propose that the origins of apocalyptic are to be found, not in the circle of prophecy, but in the Wisdom movement (see especially Gerhard von Rad, *Old Testament Theology*, Vol. II, pp. 301–308). This, however, is an extreme view that has not won wide acceptance. Apocalyptic is *prophecy in a new idiom;* but it rests on a different view of God's relation to the temporal process and specifically to the realm of politics.

One measure of the difference between prophecy and

apocalyptic is to be found in the way each uses the language of traditional mythology. Jeremiah could envision Yahweh, the Divine Warrior, coming against his own people in the guise of the Foe from the North, and could use the imagery of chaos to portray the imminence of the divine judgment (Jer. 4:23–28). In using such language, he was concerned to call the people to repentance while there was still time. But apocalyptic uses mythical language to portray a dimension of evil more terrible than anything conceived within covenant theology, with its call to human responsibility. Thus in Isa. 27:1, a passage that has striking linguistic affinities with the Canaanite myth of Baal's conflict with Yamm (Sea), we read that in the final time Yahweh will come as Divine Warrior to overcome the powers of evil.

> In that day Yahweh with his hard and great and strong sword will punish Leviathan the fleeing serpent, Leviathan the twisting serpent, and he will slay the dragon that is in the sea.

Here a new, and more radical, view of evil comes to expression. No longer is the issue "sin" and its deserved punishment, but the conquest of radical evil that infects human history itself.

Apocalyptic literature, which flourished in the period 200 B.C. to A.D. 200, is so varied that generalizations are difficult. For the purpose of our discussion it is sufficient to notice that one of its chief characteristics is a profound pessimism about the political structures and the world powers that shape and tyrannize human life (see, for instance, D. S. Russell, *The Method and Message of Jewish Apocalyptic,* and Philipp Vielhauer's contributions in Edgar Hennecke, *New Testament Apocrypha,* Vol. II). In apocalyptic the distinction be-

tween "this world [age]" and "the world [age] to come"
is not a historical distinction of the sort we would make
between an old era and a new era. Rather, the two ages
are separated by a deep qualitative gulf. According to
apocalyptic portrayal, this age is perishable and tran-
sient; the age to come will be eternal and gloriously
transfigured. This age is under the sway of demonic
powers (in the apocalyptic idiom it is under the dominion of Satan); the age to come will be the time of liberation from all the powers that dehumanize life (in the
apocalyptic idiom the Divine Warrior will win his final
victory over all the powers of darkness, chaos, and
death). This age is characterized by the moral and religious decay of humankind; the age to come will be a
time when Israel and all people will experience the
glorious liberty of the children of God. So deep is the
gulf between the two ages that human effort is ineffec-
tive in bringing about any improvement in the historical
situation. In the language of an apocalyptic tract that
was delivered to my door recently, the entire "system"
has to be shattered. And this will happen when God,
working through catastrophe, terminates the present
corrupt system and ushers in his Kingdom according to
a prearranged time schedule to which the apocalyptic
seer is made privy.

Another measure of the difference between prophecy
and apocalyptic is found in the notion of the heavenly
council, or in the sense of transcendence. The prophets,
as we have seen, understood themselves to be part of
God's cosmic administration and privy to his secret
decrees; but they considered their task to be that of
translating that vision into the concrete realities of the
political world. The apocalyptic seer also testified that
God had chosen to reveal through visions his "mys-

tery" or "secret" (*rāz,* Dan. 2:27–29). But his vision
was esoteric, communicable only to a few who could
understand its secret message. As Paul Hanson observes: "Prophetic eschatology is transformed into
apocalyptic at the point where the task of translating
the cosmic vision into the categories of mundane reality
is abdicated" ("Old Testament Apocalyptic Reexamined," in *Interpretation,* 1971; see also his *The Dawn of
Apocalyptic,* pp. 11f.).

It should not be supposed that apocalyptic is completely otherworldly and therefore politically irrele-
vant. The futuristic language of apocalyptic may serve
to evoke a radical obedience to the Torah and faithful
perseverance in the face of all hostilities. The apocalypse of Daniel was a tract for a political revolution (the
Maccabean); it provided a theological basis for a minority to make a stand with fierce zeal for the Torah, even
when all odds, politically speaking, were against them.
Understandably, apocalyptic literature has had a strong
appeal for many modern people who feel that they are
a helpless minority over against the "Establishment,"
the powers that are firmly in control. Nevertheless, this
type of literature shifts the accent from the prophetic
call for corporate repentance and social reform to an
appeal to the individual, or a small minority, to take a
stand in faith, confident that the time is near when God
will usher in the new age through a world cataclysm.
Apocalyptic characteristically calls for the virtues of
patience, long-suffering, and waiting.

Thus Israel's faith in the presence of God in history,
and specifically his activity in the political arena, was
shipwrecked on the rocks of suffering and evil. The
prophets attempted to account for Israel's sufferings in
terms of human "sin," that is, failure in covenant re-

sponsibility. In this perspective, Israel was culpable and the punishment was deserved. But apocalyptic writers knew that the sufferings of the present age could not be accounted for on the basis of deserved punishment. Too often suffering can be grotesquely out of proportion to the sins of those upon whom political tragedy has fallen —a grim fact of which our generation, which has witnessed the holocausts of Hiroshima and Auschwitz, is well aware. Faced with the power of radical evil, apocalypticists could not use the prophetic language of guilt (sin) and repentance; for they saw that human beings in general, not just Israel alone, were the *victims* of a whole system of evil that must be destroyed catastrophically if there is to be human salvation. This view is reflected in the well-known seventh chapter of Daniel, a chapter that Hal Lindsey, a popular writer on apocalyptic, acclaims as "the greatest chapter of the Old Testament" (*The Late Great Planet Earth,* pp. 90ff.). In the vision, the beasts symbolize historical evil that is unhuman in its brutality, evil that has its locus in the mysterious depths of the chaotic sea of ancient mythology, or as we might say, within the processes of history. The victory over evil, on the other hand, comes transcendently, or in mythical terms, through the figure having a human visage and coming with the clouds of heaven. God's Kingdom will come on earth, but by a radical irruption from a transcendent or heavenly source.

CHRISTIAN MODIFICATION OF APOCALYPTIC

The two perspectives that have been discussed, prophecy and apocalyptic, converge in the New Testament. The degree to which they stand in tension or are synthesized is surely one of the major issues of New Testament interpretation and, of course, one of the central concerns of Christian ethics.

It would be foolhardy to try to homogenize the writings of the New Testament into a single perspective. Nevertheless, it can scarcely be doubted that the New Testament is heavily indebted to apocalyptic categories such as the doctrine of the two ages, the kingdom of Satan, the Son of Man, and the end-time resurrection. We all know that the New Testament contains a straightforward apocalyptic writing, the Apocalypse of John, which displays striking affinities with the Book of Daniel. The thirteenth chapter of Mark is a little apocalypse, incorporated within a Gospel that in many ways is influenced by the apocalyptic perspective. And Paul's writings are imprinted with the apocalyptic view that the present age, which is under the power of evil (or the evil one), stands in radical contrast to the new age when God's victory will be consummated. This is true not only of Paul's Thessalonian correspondence but also of his magnificent eighth chapter of Romans and his exposition of resurrection-faith in I Corinthians, ch. 15.

Although various New Testament writers use the language of apocalyptic, they have profoundly modified it, so much so that it almost becomes a new way of thinking. The reason for this is to be found in what is central in the New Testament: the announcement that already God's new age has been introduced through Jesus Christ. Jesus' preaching, as reflected in the Synoptic Gospels, shows an apocalyptic orientation insofar as God's Kingdom is an act of divine intervention that brings the present evil age to an end; but *already* the Kingdom is manifest through his words and deeds. As

Philipp Vielhauer observes, the intense concentration upon the contemporary reality of God's saving presence "shatters the time-scheme of the Two-Ages doctrine" and thus obviates apocalyptic speculations about the time of the end ("Apocalyptic in Early Christianity," in Edgar Hennecke, *New Testament Apocrypha,* Vol. II, pp. 608f.). Early Christian interpreters, when elaborating the meaning of the crucifixion and resurrection of Jesus, maintained the emphasis upon the present power of God's saving presence, though not eliminating the future culmination which was conceived to be imminent. Paul, the great interpreter of the Christian story, declares that God's decisive victory over the powers of evil, chaos, and death has already occurred as an *arrabōn* or assurance of the final consummation of his purpose; hence people are invited to live in the power of that victory and, in the Spirit, to take part in his transforming work. To be sure, the "principalities and powers" are still there, but in the Christ event, God's power of love has broken through triumphantly, liberating people from impotence in the face of evil and making them "more than conquerors" (Rom. 8:31–39).

The conviction that in Christ the new age has dawned has had two important results. First, Christians have rejected a thoroughgoing Gnosticism, with its stress upon man's complete alienation from this world and his salvation from the temporal sphere. Life in this world, amid all its difficulties and perplexities, is infused with joy and hope which arise from the celebration of God's saving power in Jesus Christ, through which human history and, indeed, the whole creation are being transformed and sanctified. This world is God's world, under the signature of Jesus Christ. And second, the whole biblical story (the Law, Prophets, and Psalms) provides the context for understanding the "apocalyptic" event of the crucifixion and resurrection of Jesus Christ, and his career that leads up to that finale. When you stop to think of it, this appropriation of Israel's story is a remarkable witness to the Christian modification of apocalyptic. For apocalyptic, as represented, for instance, by the Book of Daniel, tears loose from covenantal theology and from Israel's *Heilsgeschichte.* It moves in a mythical, cosmic, and universal dimension. The New Testament writers, however, have sought in various ways to understand Jesus Christ in the context of God's working in Israel's history. Thus the witness of the prophets contributes to the understanding of the new age initiated by the resurrection of Jesus.

To be sure, Christians have found themselves living in the interim between the Already and the Not-Yet or, in Pauline terms, between the first resurrection and the final, general resurrection, of which Jesus' resurrection was a foretaste. In this interim, however, God is still working on the plane of history, as prophets once announced, to transform the world and all creation. My New Testament colleague, J. C. Beker, in a recent faculty seminar, pointed out that this is clearly the testimony of the great theologian Paul. Observing that in Pauline terms "Christian life is lived in the interim time between the two resurrections," he went on to say: "The Spirit is not simply ecstasy or the manifestation of the eternal in time; it is the power of the future kingdom breaking into the present and undergirding the sighing and hope of the Christian. The Church is not simply a gnostic society of the elite, but the avant-garde of the future kingdom in the present." He continued with words that are relevant to this essay: "The

Gospel is not simply a message aimed at the winning of souls for the Church, it is the announcement of the coming of God with his kingdom, who already claims historical reality for himself and who, since the resurrection of Christ, is engaged in destroying the hostile powers and in establishing domains of freedom in his creation" ("The Role of the Biblical Theologian in the Theological Curriculum," unpublished manuscript, Nov. 5, 1975).

IMPLICATIONS FOR POLITICAL RESPONSIBILITY

We started from the observation that American religion has been polarized into a two-party system, the "liberals" stressing God's transforming work in the social, economic, and political spheres, and the "conservatives" emphasizing individual salvation from the evils of this world. It should be apparent that these two parties may appeal to important parts of Scripture, prophecy and apocalyptic respectively. Prophetism, when taken by itself, has often degenerated into human idealism: the identification of the Kingdom of God with the society which human beings may build, either through social planning or revolutionary activity. This view is illustrated by the Christian idealists of my college generation who spoke (unbiblically) of "building the Kingdom of God on earth." Apocalyptic, when taken by itself, may lead to an abdication of political responsibility and the encouragement of individualistic morality and otherworldly piety. This view is illustrated, perhaps in extreme terms, by the evangelist Dwight L. Moody. Responding to the ills of industrial society he once said: "I look upon this world as a wrecked vessel. God has given me a lifeboat and said to me, 'Moody, save all you can!' " (quoted by Martin Marty, *Righteous Empire,* p. 184).

The relation between these two perspectives, which at first glance seem diametrically opposed, is fundamentally a problem of the biblical canon. Many Protestants are "New Testament Christians" and therefore easily fall prey to apocalypticism in its premillennial form; that is, they believe that Christ must return soon to inaugurate the millennium (see Ernest Sandeen, *The Roots of Fundamentalism*). It is significant, however, that these perspectives, which stand in uneasy tension with each other in the Bible, are brought together in the New Testament. It is not simply a matter of either prophecy or apocalyptic, for the New Testament has profoundly modified the apocalyptic perspective and therefore has reopened the message of prophecy. We need the whole canon, both Old Testament prophecy and New Testament modified apocalyptic, if we are to understand our political responsibility in the context of God's purpose for the world.

Apocalyptic presents a sharp critique of any optimistic view of history based on political action, social planning, or revolutionary zeal. In vivid language it portrays the dimension of suffering and tragedy which has been sadly lacking in the American religious heritage since the time of the Puritans. It takes seriously the radical power and universal scope of evil; for, to use apocalyptic language, the evil we wrestle with—and God wrestles with—is not mere flesh and blood, but "principalities" and "powers" (Eph. 6:12). Evil is a "demonic" power which infects institutions and runs like a cancerous network through the whole social system. People find themselves in the grip of tremendous historical forces that seduce and tyrannize, forces that we often describe as "isms": nationalism, materialism, militarism, scientism, etc. And over the whole world scene Death exerts its dominion, both for individuals and for nations or civilizations. Yet the distinctive message of apocalyptic is that the Kingdom belongs to God, and he inaugurates his rule in his own way and in his own time.

The New Testament picks up at this point with its announcement of God's "apocalyptic" victory in Jesus Christ over all the powers of evil, darkness, and death. This good news, however, provides a new motivation for political responsibility in the prophetic perspective. "If God be for us, who then can be against us?" Paul exclaimed in a triumphant passage in Rom., ch. 8. In the interim between the Decisive Victory and the Final Consummation, between the Already and the Not-Yet, God calls his people not only to announce the good news to the nations but to act responsibly in society, thereby fulfilling prophecy with its covenant promises and demands. This is the way early American Puritans understood Scripture, according to Gordon Harland, a perceptive interpreter of American church history. They came to the New Land with the conviction that "God was using his 'saints' as his chosen 'instrument' to revolutionize human history." They were conscious of "the tragic dimension" of history, that is, "the depth, subtlety, and pervasiveness of sin," but they also knew, like the prophets and the apostles, "the wondrous working of grace." Accordingly, they sought to bring family life, church, and government under the "ordering principle" of the covenant, with its prophetic demand to "do justice, love mercy, and walk humbly with God" (Micah 6:8) ("The American Religious Heritage and the Tragic Dimension," in *Studies in Religion,* 1973).

This biblical vision of political responsibility, too often obscured by civil religion or otherworldly piety, was eloquently expressed by Abraham Lincoln, whom Gordon Harland rightly acclaims as "the spiritual center of American history." Lincoln had a lively awareness of the action of God in the concrete and tragic situations of American history. "The Almighty has his own purposes"—which are not commensurate with human intentions, and therefore decisions must be made with an uneasy conscience, subject to the judgment and the mercy of God. The God of the prophets not only calls his people to seek out "the ancient paths" (Jer. 6:16) which have been forgotten, but he is the innovating God who does the new thing. He introduces an element of "divine surprise" into history. Hence the politician who has biblical insight will measure "what is possible" against the vision of what God has done and is doing, even though this may mean taking calculated risks which go beyond what is politically expedient. Was this not Lincoln's attitude? In political debate he could take a firm stand based on political realities. To a group of Chicago clergymen, who visited him before the announcement of the Emancipation Proclamation and sought to show that the Bible supported him, he insisted that his decision could not be based on "direct revelation," but only upon a measurement of "the plain physical facts of the case" (Elton Trueblood, *Abraham Lincoln,* pp. 53f.). But his vision of God's transcendence prompted him to take political risks that went beyond merely pragmatic considerations and to advocate amnesty and reconciliation "with malice toward none, with charity for all." If God is really doing something *new* which may outshine all that has gone before, as the prophets insisted, why should anyone underestimate the creative possibilities in the political situation?

In conclusion, both prophecy and apocalyptic call us to political responsibility. To be sure, the Bible does not give us a political program or a guarantee of success. It only enables us to view political responsibility in the dimension of God's transcendence. If, however, we share the perspectives of prophecy and apocalyptic, we will see ourselves as participants in a wonderful drama of redemption that is enacted in human history. And despite all obstacles and the entrenched power of evil we will respond faithfully to the word of an apostle, spoken at the end of an apocalyptic passage: "Be steadfast, immovable, always abounding in the work of the Lord, knowing that in the Lord your labor is not in vain" (I Cor. 15:58). Or, in the language of Lincoln, "With firmness in the right as God gives us to see the right, let us strive on to finish the work we are in," knowing that the ultimate outcome of our actions is in the hand of God.

Bibliographical References

Anderson, Bernhard W. "Exodus and Covenant in Second Isaiah and Prophetic Tradition," in George Ernest Wright, *Magnalia Dei: The Mighty Acts of God: Essays on the Bible and Archaeology in Memory of G. Ernest Wright,* ed. by F. M. Cross *et al.* Doubleday & Company, Inc., 1976. Pp. 339–360.

————. "Exodus Typology in Second Isaiah," in *Israel's Prophetic Heritage,* ed. by Bernhard W. Anderson and Walter Harrelson. Harper & Row, Publishers, Inc., 1962. Pp. 177–196.

————. "Human Dominion Over Nature," in *Biblical Studies in Contemporary Thought,* ed. by Miriam Ward. Greeno, Hadden & Co., Ltd., 1975. Pp. 27–45.

————. "Politics and the Transcendent: Voegelin's Philosophical and Theological Exposition of the Old Testament in the Context of the Ancient Near East," in *Eric Voegelin's Search for Order in History,* ed. by Stephen A. McKnight. Louisiana State University Press, 1978. Pp. 62–100.

Auerbach, Erich. *Mimesis: The Representation of Reality in Western Literature,* tr. by Willard Trask. Doubleday & Company, Inc., 1957.

Barr, James. *The Bible in the Modern World.* Harper & Row, Publishers, Inc., 1973.

————. "Revelation in History," in *The Interpreter's Dictionary of the Bible,* Supplementary Volume, ed. by Keith Crim. Abingdon Press, 1976. Pp. 746–749.

————. "Revelation Through History in the Old Testament and in Modern Theology," 1962 Inaugural Address, *Interpretation,* Vol. 17 (1963), pp. 193–205.

Barth, Karl. *Church Dogmatics,* Vol. I, Pt. 1, tr. by G. T. Thomson. Edinburgh: T. & T. Clark, 1936.

Beker, J. C. "The Role of the Biblical Theologian in the Theological Curriculum." A paper presented to the Faculty Seminar, Princeton Theological Seminary, Nov. 5, 1975.

Buber, Martin. *Eclipse of God: Studies in the Relation Between Religion and Philosophy.* Harper & Brothers, 1952.

————. *Moses: The Revelation and the Covenant.* Harper & Brothers, 1958.

Childs, Brevard. *Biblical Theology in Crisis.* The Westminster Press, 1970.

Coats, George W. "Abraham's Sacrifice of Faith: A Form-Critical Study of Genesis 22," *Interpretation,* Vol. 27 (1973), pp. 389–400.

Constitution of The United Presbyterian Church in the U.S.A. Office of the General Assembly, 1966.

Ebeling, Gerhard. *Word and Faith,* tr. by James A. Leitch. Fortress Press, 1963.

Fackenheim, Emil. *God's Presence in History: Jewish Affirmations and Philosophical Reflections.* New York University Press, 1970.

Fokkelman, J. P. *Narrative Art in Genesis: Specimens of Stylistic and Structural Analysis.* Amsterdam: Van Gorcum, 1975.

Frye, Northrop. *A Natural Perspective: The Development of Shakespearean Comedy and Romance.* Columbia University Press, 1965.

Gabler, J. P. "Oratio de iusto discrimine theologiae biblicae et dogmaticae regundisque utriusque finibus." Inaugural Address printed in his *Opuscula Academica,* 2 (Altdorf: G. P. Monath, 1787), pp. 179–198. English translation: "A Discourse on the Proper Distinction Between Biblical and Dogmatic Theology and the Boundaries to Be Drawn for Each," tr. by Karlfried Froehlich, Speer Library manuscript, Princeton Theological Seminary.

Gilkey, Langdon. "Cosmology, Ontology, and the Travail of Biblical Language," *Journal of Religion,* Vol. 41 (1961), pp. 194–205.

Graham, Billy. "A Clarification," *Christianity Today,* Vol. 17 (1972–1973), p. 416.

Gutiérrez, Gustavo. *A Theology of Liberation,* tr. and ed. by Caridad Inda and John Eagleson. Orbis Books, 1973.

Hanson, Paul D. *The Dawn of Apocalyptic.* Fortress Press, 1975.

———. "Old Testament Apocalyptic Reexamined," *Interpretation,* Vol. 25 (1971), pp. 454–479.

Harland, Gordon. "The American Religious Heritage and the Tragic Dimension," *Studies in Religion,* Vol. 2 (1973), pp. 277–288.

Hendry, George S. "The Theology of Nature." A paper presented to the Faculty Seminar, Princeton Theological Seminary, Jan. 17, 1974.

Herberg, Will. *Faith Enacted as History,* ed. and with an introduction by Bernhard W. Anderson. The Westminster Press, 1976.

Heschel, Abraham. *Between God and Man: An Inter-*

pretation of Judaism, ed. and with an introduction by
F. A. Rothschild. Free Press, 1965.

―――. "A Conversation with Dr. Abraham Joshua
Heschel," presented by the National Broadcasting
Company under the auspices of the Jewish Theologi-
cal Seminary of America on Feb. 4, 1973.

Hillers, Delbert. *Covenant: The History of a Biblical
Idea.* Johns Hopkins Press, 1969.

Keller, Werner. *Und die Bibel hat doch Recht.* English
translation: *The Bible as History: A Confirmation of
the Book of Books,* tr. by William Neil (William Mor-
row & Co., Inc., 1956).

Lindsell, Harold. *The Battle for the Bible.* Zondervan
Publishing House, 1976.

Lindsey, Hal. *The Late Great Planet Earth.* Zondervan
Publishing House, 1970.

McCarthy, Dennis J., S.J. *Old Testament Covenant: A
Survey of Current Opinions.* John Knox Press, 1972.

Maier, Gerhard. *The End of the Historical-Critical
Method,* tr. by E. W. Leverenz and R. F. Norden.
Concordia Publishing House, 1977.

Marty, Martin E. *Righteous Empire: The Protestant
Experience in America.* Dial Press, 1970.

Migliore, Daniel. "Scripture as Liberating Word." A
paper presented to the Faculty Seminar, Princeton
Theological Seminary, March 1978.

Miranda, José. *Marx and the Bible: A Critique of the
Philosophy of Oppression,* tr. by John Eagleson. Orbis
Books, 1974.

Murphy, Roland. "The Old Testament as Word of
God," in *A Light Unto My Path: Old Testament Studies in Honor of Jacob M. Myers,* ed. by H. N. Bream
et al. Temple University Press, 1974. Pp. 363–374.

Niebuhr, H. Richard. *The Meaning of Revelation.* The Macmillan Company, 1941.

Noth, Martin. *History of Pentateuchal Traditions,* tr. and with an introduction by Bernhard W. Anderson. Prentice-Hall, Inc., 1972.

Orwell, George. *Animal Farm.* Harcourt, Brace and Company, Inc., 1946.

Otto, Rudolf. *Das Heilige: über das Irrational in der Idee des Göttlichen und sein Verhältnis zum Rationalen* (Breslau: Trewendt und Granier, 1923). English translation: *The Idea of the Holy: An Inquiry Into the Non-rational Factor in the Idea of the Divine and Its Relation to the Rational,* tr. by J. W. Harvey (London: Oxford University Press, 1923).

Pedersen, Johannes. *Israel: Its Life and Culture,* Vol. III–IV. London: Oxford University Press, 1947.

Rad, Gerhard von. *Old Testament Theology,* 2 vols. Tr. by D. M. G. Stalker. Harper & Row, Publishers, Inc., 1962, 1965.

Russell, D. S. *The Method and Message of Jewish Apocalyptic.* The Westminster Press, 1964.

Sandeen, Ernest R. *The Roots of Fundamentalism: British-American Millenarianism.* The University of Chicago Press, 1970.

Smith, George Adam. *Modern Criticism and the Preaching of the Old Testament.* London: Hodder & Stoughton, 1901.

Speiser, E. A. *Genesis* (The Anchor Bible). Doubleday & Company, Inc., 1964.

Stuhlmacher, Peter. *Historical Criticism and Theological Interpretation of Scripture: Toward a Hermeneutics of Consent,* tr. and with an introduction by Roy A. Harrisville. Fortress Press, 1977.

Troeltsch, Ernst. "Über historische und dogmatische Methode in der Theologie," in *Gesammelte Schriften,* Bd. II. Tübingen: J. C. B. Mohr (Paul Siebeck), 1913. Pp. 728–753.

Trueblood, Elton. *Abraham Lincoln: Theologian of American Anguish.* Harper & Row, Publishers, Inc., 1973.

Vielhauer, Philipp. "Apocalypses and Related Subjects," in Edgar Hennecke, *New Testament Apocrypha,* Vol. II: *Writings Relating to the Apostles; Apocalypses and Related Subjects,* ed. by Wilhelm Schneemelcher; English translation ed. by R. McL. Wilson. The Westminster Press, 1965. Pp. 579–607.

———. "Apocalyptic in Early Christianity: Introduction," in *New Testament Apocrypha,* Vol. II, pp. 608–642.

Voegelin, Eric. *Israel and Revelation.* Louisiana State University Press, 1956.

Weber, Max. *Ancient Judaism,* tr. by Hans H. Gerth and Don Martindale. The Free Press, 1952.

White, Lynn. "The Historical Roots of Our Ecologic Crisis," *Science,* Vol. 155 (1967), pp. 1203–1207. Reprinted in *The Environmental Handbook,* ed. by Garrett DeBell. Ballantine Books, Inc., 1970. Pp. 12–26.

Wilder, Amos. *Early Christian Rhetoric: The Language of the Gospel* (Harvard University Press, 1971). First edition: *The Language of the Gospel* (London: SCM Press, Ltd., 1964).

Wolff, Hans Walter. "The Elohistic Fragments in the Pentateuch," in *The Vitality of Old Testament Traditions,* by H. W. Wolff and Walter Brueggemann. John Knox Press, 1975. Pp. 67–82.

Wright, George Ernest. *God Who Acts: Biblical Theol-*

ogy as Recital (Studies in Biblical Theology, 8). London: SCM Press, Ltd., 1952.

————. *Magnalia Dei: The Mighty Acts of God: Essays on the Bible and Archaeology in Memory of G. Ernest Wright,* ed. by F. M. Cross, W. E. Lemke, and Patrick D. Miller. Doubleday & Company, Inc., 1976.

————. "The Nations in Hebrew Prophecy," *Encounter,* Vol. 25 (1965), pp. 225–237.

Wright, George Ernest, and Fuller, Reginald H. *The Book of the Acts of God: Christian Scholarship Interprets the Bible.* Doubleday & Company, Inc., 1957.